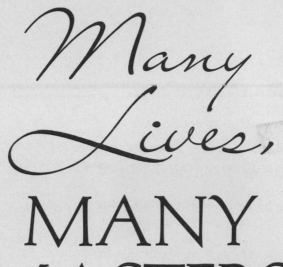

Many Lives, MANY MASTERS

The True Story of a Prominent
Psychiatrist, His Young Patient,
and the Past-Life Therapy That
Changed Both Their Lives

BRIAN L. WEISS, M.D.

D0068224

A FIRESIDE BOOK
Published by Simon & Schuster
New York   London   Toronto   Sydney

FIRESIDE
Rockefeller Center
1230 Avenue of the Americas
New York, NY 10020

Copyright © 1988 by Brian L. Weiss, M.D.
All rights reserved,
including the right of reproduction
in whole or in part in any form.

FIRESIDE and colophon are registered trademarks
of Simon & Schuster, Inc.

For information about special discounts for bulk purchases,
please contact Simon & Schuster Special Sales:
1-800-456-6798 or business@simonandschuster.com.

Designed by Kathy Kikkert

Manufactured in the United States of America

50   49   48   47   46   45

Library of Congress Cataloging-in-Publication Data
Weiss, Brian L. (Brian Leslie).
   Many lives, many masters.
   "A Fireside book."
      1. Catherine, 1952 or 3–   . 2. Reincarnation—
Biography.   3. Weiss, Brian L. (Brian Leslie).
4. Reincarnation therapy.   I. Title.
BL520.C37W45   1988   133.9'01'3 [B]   87-34323

ISBN-13: 978-0-671-65786-4
ISBN-10:   0-671-65786-0

Also by Brian Weiss

Same Soul, Many Bodies: Discover the Healing Power of Future Lives Through Progression Therapy

Eliminating Stress, Finding Inner Peace

Mirrors of Time: Using Regression for Physical, Emotional, and Spiritual Healing

Messages from the Masters: Tapping into the Power of Love

Only Love Is Real: A Story of Soulmates Reunited

Through Time into Healing

To Carole, my wife,
Whose love has nourished and sustained me
for longer than I can remember.

We are together, to the end of time.

My thanks and love go to my children, Jordan and Amy, who forgave me for stealing so much time from them to write this book.

I also thank Nicole Paskow for transcribing the audiotapes of the therapy sessions.

Julie Rubin's editorial suggestions after reading the first draft of this book were most valuable.

My heartfelt thanks go to Barbara Gess, my editor at Simon & Schuster, for her expertise and her courage.

My deep appreciation goes to all of the others, here and there, who have made this book possible.

PREFACE

I know that there is a reason for everything. Perhaps at the moment that an event occurs we have neither the insight nor the foresight to comprehend the reason, but with time and patience it will come to light.

So it was with Catherine. I first met her in 1980 when she was twenty-seven years old. She had come to my office seeking help for her anxiety, panic attacks, and phobias. Although these symptoms had been with her since childhood, in the recent past they had become much worse. Every day she found herself more emotionally paralyzed and less able to function. She was terrified and understandably depressed.

In contrast to the chaos that was going on in her life at that time, my life was flowing smoothly. I had a good stable marriage, two young children, and a flourishing career.

From the beginning, my life seemed always to have been on a straight course. I had grown up in a loving home. Academic success had come easily, and by my sophomore year in college I had made the decision to become a psychiatrist.

I was graduated Phi Beta Kappa, magna cum laude, from Columbia University in New York in 1966. I then went to the Yale University School of Medicine and received my M.D. degree in 1970. Following an internship at the New York University-Bellevue Medical Center, I returned to Yale to complete my residency in psychiatry. Upon completion, I accepted a faculty position at the University of Pittsburgh. Two years later, I joined the faculty of the University of Miami, heading the psychopharmacology division. There I achieved national recognition in the fields of biological psychiatry and substance abuse. After four years at the university, I was promoted to the rank of Associate Professor of Psychiatry at the medical school, and I was appointed Chief of Psychiatry at a large university-affiliated hospital in Miami. By that time, I had already published thirty-seven scientific papers and book chapters in my field.

Years of disciplined study had trained my mind to think as a scientist and physician, molding me along the narrow paths of conservatism in my profession. I distrusted anything that could not be proved by traditional scientific methods. I was aware of some of the studies in parapsychology that were being conducted at major universities across the country, but they did not hold my attention. It all seemed too farfetched to me.

Then I met Catherine. For eighteen months I used conventional methods of therapy to help her overcome her symptoms. When nothing seemed to work, I tried hypnosis. In a series of trance states, Catherine recalled "past-life" memories that proved to be the causative factors of her symptoms. She also was able to act as a conduit for information from highly evolved "spirit entities," and through them she revealed many of the secrets of life and of death. In just a few short months, her symptoms disappeared, and she resumed her life, happier and more at peace than ever before.

Nothing in my background had prepared me for this. I was absolutely amazed when these events unfolded.

I do not have a scientific explanation for what happened. There is far too much about the human mind that is beyond our comprehension. Perhaps, under hypnosis, Catherine was able to focus in on the part of her subconscious mind that stored actual past-life memories, or perhaps she had tapped into what the psychoanalyst Carl Jung termed the collective unconscious, the energy source that surrounds us and contains the memories of the entire human race.

Scientists are beginning to seek these answers. We, as a society, have much to gain from research into the mysteries of the mind, the soul, the continuation of life after death, and the influence of our past-life experiences on our present behavior. Obviously, the ramifications are limitless, particularly in the fields of medicine, psychiatry, theology, and philosophy.

However, scientifically rigorous research in this area is in its infancy. Strides are being made to uncover this information, but the process is slow and is met with much resistance by scientists and lay people alike.

Throughout history, humankind has been resistant to change and to the acceptance of new ideas. Historical lore is replete with examples. When Galileo discovered the moons of Jupiter, the astronomers of that time refused to accept or even to look at these satellites because the existence of these moons conflicted with their accepted beliefs. So it is now with psychiatrists and other therapists, who refuse to examine and evaluate the considerable evidence being gathered about survival after bodily death and about past-life memories. Their eyes stay tightly shut.

This book is my small contribution to the ongoing research in the field of parapsychology, especially the branch dealing with our experiences before birth and after death. Every word that you will be reading is true. I have added nothing, and I have deleted only those parts that were repetitious. I have slightly changed Catherine's identity to ensure confidentiality.

It took me four years to write about what happened, four

years to garner the courage to take the professional risk of revealing this unorthodox information.

Suddenly one night while I was taking a shower, I felt compelled to put this experience down on paper. I had a strong feeling that the time was right, that I should not withhold the information any longer. The lessons I had learned were meant to be shared with others, not to be kept private. The knowledge had come through Catherine and now had to come through me. I knew that no possible consequence I might face could prove to be as devastating as not sharing the knowledge I had gained about immortality and the true meaning of life.

I rushed out of the shower and sat down at my desk with the stack of audio tapes I had made during my sessions with Catherine. In the wee hours of the morning, I thought of my old Hungarian grandfather who had died while I was still a teenager. Whenever I would tell him that I was afraid to take a risk, he would lovingly encourage me by repeating his favorite English expression: "Vat the hell," he would say, "vat the hell."

Chapter
ONE

The first time I saw Catherine she was wearing a vivid crimson dress and was nervously leafing through a magazine in my waiting room. She was visibly out of breath. For the previous twenty minutes she had been pacing the corridor outside the Department of Psychiatry offices, trying to convince herself to keep her appointment with me and not run away.

I went out to the waiting room to greet her, and we shook hands. I noticed that hers were cold and damp, confirming her anxiety. Actually, it had taken her two months of courage-gathering to make an appointment to see me even though she had been strongly advised to seek my help by two staff physicians, both of whom she trusted. Finally, she was here.

Catherine is an extraordinarily attractive woman, with medium-length blond hair and hazel eyes. At that time, she worked as a laboratory technician in the hospital where I was Chief of Psychiatry, and she earned extra money modeling swimwear.

I ushered her into my office, past the couch and to a large leather chair. We sat across from each other, my semicircular desk separating us. Catherine leaned back in her chair, silent, not knowing where to begin. I waited, preferring that she choose the opening, but after a few minutes I began inquiring about her past. On that first visit we began to unravel who she was and why she had come to see me.

In answer to my questions, Catherine revealed the story of her life. She was the middle child, reared in a conservative Catholic family in a small Massachusetts town. Her brother, born three years earlier than she, was very athletic, and he enjoyed a freedom that she was never allowed. Her younger sister was the favorite of both parents.

When we started to talk about her symptoms, she became noticeably more tense and nervous. Her speech was rapid, and she leaned forward, resting her elbows on the desk. Her life had always been burdened with fears. She feared water, feared choking to the extent that she could not swallow pills, feared airplanes, feared the dark, and she was terrified of dying. In the recent past, her fears had begun to worsen. In order to feel safe, she often slept in the walk-in closet in her apartment. She suffered two to three hours of insomnia before being able to fall alseep. Once asleep, she would sleep lightly and fitfully, awakening frequently. The nightmares and sleep-walking episodes that had plagued her childhood were returning. As her fears and symptoms increasingly paralyzed her, she became more and more depressed.

As Catherine continued to talk, I could sense how deeply she was suffering. Over the years I had helped many patients like Catherine through the agonies of their fears, and I felt confident that I could help her, too. I decided we would begin by delving into her childhood, looking for the original sources of her problems. Usually this kind of insight helps to alleviate anxiety. If necessary, and if she could manage to swallow pills, I would offer her some mild anti-anxiety medications to make her more comfortable. This was standard textbook treatment for Catherine's symptoms, and I never hesitated to use tranquilizers, or even antidepressant medicines, to treat chronic, severe fears and anxieties. Now I use these medicines much more sparingly and only temporarily, if at all. No medicine can reach the real roots of these symptoms. My experiences with Catherine and others like her have proved this to me. Now I know there can be cures, not just the suppression or covering-over of symptoms.

During the first session, I kept trying to gently nudge her back to her childhood. Because Catherine remembered amazingly few events from her early years, I made a mental note to consider hypnotherapy as a possible shortcut to overcome this repression. She could not remember any particularly traumatic moments in her childhood that would explain the epidemic of fears in her life.

As she strained and stretched her mind to remember, isolated memory fragments emerged. When she was about five years old, she had panicked when someone had pushed her off a diving board into a swimming pool. She said that even before that incident, however, she had never felt comfortable in water. When Catherine was eleven, her mother had become severely depressed. Her mother's strange withdrawal from the family necessitated visits to a psychiatrist with ensuing electroshock treatments. These treatments had made it difficult for her mother to remember things. This experience with her mother frightened Catherine, but, as her mother improved and became "herself" again, Catherine said that her fears dissipated. Her father had a long-standing history of alcohol abuse, and sometimes Catherine's brother had to retrieve their father from the local bar. Her father's increasing alcohol consumption led to his having frequent fights with her mother, who would then become moody and withdrawn. However, Catherine viewed this as an accepted family pattern.

Things were better outside the home. She dated in high school and mixed in easily with her friends, most of whom she had known for many years. However, she found it difficult to trust people, especially those outside her small circle of friends.

Her religion was simple and unquestioned. She was raised to believe in traditional Catholic ideology and practices, and she had never really doubted the truthfulness and validity of her faith. She believed that if you were a good Catholic and lived properly by observing the faith and its rituals, you would be rewarded by going to heaven; if not, you would experience purgatory or hell. A patriarchal God and his Son made these final decisions. I later learned that Catherine did not believe in reincarnation; in fact, she knew very little about the concept, although she had read sparingly about the Hindus. Reincarnation was an idea contrary to her upbringing and understanding. She had never read any metaphysical or occult literature, having had no interest in it. She was secure in her beliefs.

After high school, Catherine completed a two-year technical program, emerging as a laboratory technician. Armed with a profession and encouraged by her brother's move to Tampa, Catherine landed a job in Miami at a large teaching hospital affiliated with the University of Miami School of Medicine. She moved to Miami in the spring of 1974, at the age of twenty-one.

Catherine's life in a small town had been easier than her life in Miami turned out to be, yet she was glad she had fled her family problems.

During her first year in Miami, Catherine met Stuart. Married, Jewish, and with two children, he was totally different from any other man she had ever dated. He was a successful physician, strong and aggressive. There was an irresistible chemistry between them, but their affair was rocky and tempestuous. Something about him drew out her passions and awakened her, as if she were charmed by him. At the time Catherine started therapy, her affair with Stuart was in its sixth year and very much alive, if not well. Catherine could not resist Stuart although he treated her poorly, and she was furious at his lies, broken promises, and manipulations.

Several months prior to her appointment with me, Catherine had required vocal cord surgery for a benign nodule. She had been anxious prior to the surgery but was absolutely terrified upon awakening in the recovery room. It took hours for the nursing staff to calm her. After her recovery in the hospital, she sought out Dr. Edward Poole. Ed was a kindly pediatrician whom Catherine had met while working in the hospital. They had both felt an instant rapport and had developed a close friendship. Catherine talked freely to Ed, telling him of her fears, her relationship with Stuart, and that she felt she was losing control over her life. He insisted that she make an appointment with me and only me, not with any of my associate psychiatrists. When Ed called to tell me about his referral, he explained that, for some reason, he thought only I could truly understand Catherine, even though the other psychiatrists also had excellent credentials and were skilled therapists. Catherine did not call me, however.

Eight weeks passed. In the crunch of my busy practice as head of the Department of Psychiatry, I had forgotten about Ed's call. Catherine's fears and phobias worsened. Dr. Frank Acker, Chief of Surgery, had known Catherine casually for years, and they often bantered good-naturedly when he visited the laboratory where she worked. He had noticed her recent unhappiness and sensed her tension. Several times he had meant to say something to her but had hesitated. One afternoon, Frank was driving to a smaller, out-of-the way hospital to give a lecture. On the way, he saw Catherine driving to her home, which was close to that hospital, and impulsively waved her to the side of the road. "I want you to see Dr. Weiss *now*," he yelled through the window. "No delays." Although surgeons often act impulsively, even Frank was surprised at how emphatic he was.

Catherine's panic attacks and anxiety were increasing in frequency and duration. She began having two recurrent nightmares. In one, a bridge collapsed while she was driving across it. Her car plunged into the water below, and she was trapped and drowning. In the second dream, she was trapped in a pitch-black room, stumbling and falling over things, unable to find a way out. Finally, she came to see me.

At the time of my first session with Catherine, I had no idea that my life was about to turn upside down, that the frightened, confused woman across the desk from me would be the catalyst, and that I would never be the same again.

Chapter
TWO

Eighteen months of intensive psychotherapy passed, with Catherine coming to see me once or twice a week. She was a good patient, verbal, capable of insights, and extremely eager to get well.

During that time, we explored her feelings, thoughts, and dreams. Her recognition of recurrent behavior patterns provided her with insight and understanding. She remembered many more significant details from her past, such as her merchant seaman father's absences from the home and his occasional violent outbursts after drinking too much. She understood much more about her turbulent relationship with Stuart, and she expressed anger more appropriately. I felt that she should have been much improved by now. Patients almost always improve when they remember unpleasant influences from their past, when they learn to recognize and correct maladaptive behavior patterns, and when they develop insight and view their problems from a larger, more detached perspective. But Catherine had not improved.

Anxiety and panic attacks still tortured her. The vivid recurrent nightmares continued, and she was still terrified of the dark, of water, and of being closed in. Her sleep was still fragmented and unrefreshing. She was experiencing heart palpitations. She continued to refuse any medicines, afraid of

23

choking on the pills. I felt as if I had reached a wall, and that no matter what I did, that wall would remain so high that neither of us would be able to climb over it. But, with my sense of frustration came an added sense of determination. Somehow, I was going to help Catherine.

And then a strange thing happened. Although she was intensely afraid of flying and had to fortify herself with several drinks while she was on the plane, Catherine accompanied Stuart to a medical conference in Chicago in the spring of 1982. While there, she pressured him into visiting the Egyptian exhibit at the art museum, where they joined a guided tour.

Catherine had always had an interest in ancient Egyptian artifacts and reproductions of relics from that period. She was hardly a scholar and had never studied that time in history, but somehow the pieces seemed familiar to her.

When the guide began to describe some of the artifacts in the exhibit, she found herself correcting him . . . and she was right! The guide was surprised; Catherine was stunned. How did she know these things? Why did she feel so strongly that *she* was right, so sure of herself that she corrected the guide in public? Perhaps the memories were forgotten from her childhood.

At her next appointment, she told me what had happened. Months earlier I had suggested hypnosis to Catherine, but she was afraid and she resisted. Because of her experience at the Egyptian exhibit, she now reluctantly agreed.

Hypnosis is an excellent tool to help a patient remember long-forgotten incidents. There is nothing mysterious about it. It is just a state of focused concentration. Under the instruction of a trained hypnotist, the patient's body relaxes, causing the memory to sharpen. I had hypnotized hundreds of patients and had found it helpful in reducing anxiety, eliminating phobias, changing bad habits, and aiding in the recall of repressed material. On occasion, I had been successful in regressing patients back to their early childhoods, even to when they were two or three years old, thus eliciting the memories of long-forgotten traumas that were disrupting their lives. I felt confident that hypnosis would help Catherine.

I instructed Catherine to lie on the couch with her eyes slightly closed and her head resting on a small pillow. At first we focused on her breathing. With each exhalation she released stored-up tension and anxiety; with each inhalation she relaxed even more. After several minutes of this, I told her to visualize her muscles progressively relaxing, beginning with her facial muscles and jaw, then her neck and shoulders, her arms, back and stomach muscles, and finally her legs. She felt her entire body sinking deeper and deeper into the couch.

Then I instructed her to visualize a bright white light at the top of her head, inside her body. Later on, as I had the light spread slowly down her body, it completely relaxed every muscle, every nerve, every organ—all of her body—bringing her into a deeper and deeper state of relaxation and peace. She felt sleepier and sleepier, more and more peaceful and calm. Eventually, at my instruction, the light filled her body and surrounded her as well.

I counted backward slowly from ten to one. With each number, she entered a deeper level of relaxation. Her trance state deepened. She was able to concentrate on my voice and exclude all background noises. By the count of one, she was already in a moderately deep state of hypnosis. The entire process had taken about twenty minutes.

After a while I began to regress her, asking her to recall memories of progressively earlier ages. She was able to talk and to answer my questions while maintaining a deep level of hypnosis. She remembered a traumatic experience at the dentist that occurred when she was six years old. She vividly remembered the terrifying experience at age five when she was pushed from a diving board into a pool. She had gagged and choked then, swallowing some water, and while talking about it she began to gag in my office. I suggested to her that the experience was over, that she was out of the water. The gagging stopped, and she resumed her normal breathing. She was still in a deep trance.

At age three, the worst event of all had occurred. She remembered awakening in her dark bedroom and being aware that her father was in her room. He reeked of alcohol then, and she could smell it now. He touched her and rubbed her, even "down there." She was terrified and began to cry, so he covered her mouth with his rough hand. She could not breathe. In my office, on my couch, twenty-five years later, Catherine began to sob. I felt that we had the information now, the key to the lock. I was sure that her symptoms would improve quickly and dramatically. I softly suggested to her that the experience was over, that she was no longer in her bedroom but was resting quietly, still in a trance. The sobbing ended. I took her forward in time to her current age. I awakened her after I had instructed her, by posthypnotic suggestion, to remember all that she had told me. We spent the remainder of the session discussing her suddenly vivid memory of the trauma with her father. I tried to help her accept and integrate her "new" knowledge. She now understood her relationship with her father, his reactions to her, his aloofness, and her fear of him. She was still shaking when she left the office, but I knew the understanding she had gained was worth the momentary discomfort.

In the drama of uncovering her painful and deeply repressed memories, I had entirely forgotten to look for the possible childhood connection to her knowledge of the Egyptian artifacts. But at least she understood more about her past. She had remembered several terrifying events, and I expected a significant improvement in her symptoms.

Despite this new understanding, the next week she reported that her symptoms remained intact, as severe as ever. I was surprised. I could not understand what was wrong. Could something have happened earlier than age three? We had uncovered more than sufficient reasons for her fear of choking, of the water, of the dark, and of being trapped, and yet the piercing fears and symptoms, the uncontrolled anxiety, were all still devastating her waking moments. Her nightmares were as terrifying as before. I decided to regress her further.

While hypnotized, Catherine spoke in a slow and deliberate whisper. Because of this, I was able to write down her words verbatim and have quoted Catherine directly. (The ellipses represent pauses in her speech, not deletions of words nor editing on my part. However, some of the material that is repetitious is not included here.)

Slowly, I took Catherine back to the age of two, but she recalled no significant memories. I instructed her firmly and clearly: "Go back to the time from which your symptoms arise." I was totally unprepared for what came next.

"I see white steps leading up to a building, a big white building with pillars, open in front. There are no doorways. I'm wearing a long dress . . . a sack made of rough material. My hair is braided, long blond hair."

I was confused. I wasn't sure what was happening. I asked her what the year was, what her name was. "Aronda . . . I am eighteen. I see a marketplace in front of the building. There are baskets. . . . You carry the baskets on your shoulders. We live in a valley. . . . There is no water. The year is 1863 B.C. The area is barren, hot, and sandy. There is a well, no rivers. Water comes into the valley from the mountains."

After she related more topographical details, I told her to go several years ahead in time and to tell me what she saw.

"There are trees and a stone road. I see a fire with cooking. My hair is blond. I'm wearing a long, coarse brown dress and sandals. I am twenty-five. I have a girl child whose name is Cleastra. . . . She's Rachel. [Rachel is presently her niece; they have always had an extremely close relationship.] It's very hot."

I was startled. My stomach knotted, and the room felt cold. Her visualizations and recall seemed so definite. She was not at all tentative. Names, dates, clothes, trees—all seen vividly! What was going on here? How could the child she had then be her niece now? I was even more confused. I had examined thousands of psychiatric patients, many under hypnosis, and I had never come across fantasies like this before—not even in dreams. I instructed her to go forward to the time of her death. I wasn't sure how to interview someone in the middle of such an explicit fantasy (or memory?), but I was on the lookout for traumatic events that might underlie current fears or symptoms. The events around the time of death could be particularly traumatic. Apparently a flood or tidal wave was devastating the village.

"There are big waves knocking down trees. There's no place to run. It's cold; the water is cold. I have to save my baby, but I cannot . . . just have to hold her tight. I drown; the water chokes me. I can't breathe, can't swallow . . . salty water. My baby is torn out of my arms." Catherine was gasping and having difficulty breathing. Suddenly her body relaxed completely, and her breathing became deep and even.

"I see clouds. . . . My baby is with me. And others from my village. I see my brother."

She was resting; this lifetime had ended. She was still in a deep trance. I was stunned! Previous lifetimes? Reincarnation? My clinical mind told me that she was not fantasizing this material, that she was not making this up. Her thoughts, her expressions, the attention to particular details, all were different from her conscious state. The whole gamut of possible psychiatric diagnoses flashed through my mind, but her psychiatric state and her character structure did not explain these revelations. Schizophrenia? No, she had never had any evidence of a cognitive or thinking disorder. She had never experienced any auditory hallucinations of hearing voices, visual hallucinations or visions while awake, or any other type of psychotic episodes. She was not delusional, nor was she out of touch with reality. She did not have multiple or split personalities. There was only one Catherine, and her conscious mind was totally aware of this. She had no sociopathic or antisocial tendencies. She was not an actress. She did not use drugs, nor did she ingest hallucinogenic substances. Her use of alcohol was minimal. She had no neurological or psychological illnesses that could explain this vivid, immediate experience while hypnotized.

These were memories of some sort, but from where? My gut reaction was that I had stumbled upon something I knew very little about—reincarnation and past-life memories. It couldn't be, I told myself; my scientifically trained mind resisted it. Yet here it was, happening right before my eyes. I couldn't explain it, but I couldn't deny the reality of it either.

"Go on," I said, a little unnerved but fascinated by what was happening. "Do you remember anything else?" She remembered fragments of two other lifetimes.

"I have on a dress with black lace, and there is black lace on my head. I have dark hair with gray in it. It's [A.D.] 1756. I am Spanish. My name is Louisa and I'm fifty-six. I'm dancing; others are dancing, too. [Long pause] I'm sick; I have a fever, cold sweats. . . . Lots of people are sick; people are dying. . . . The doctors don't know it was from the water." I took her ahead in time. "I recover, but my head still hurts; my eyes and head still hurt from the fever, from the water. . . . Many die."

Later she told me that she was a prostitute in that lifetime, but she had not relayed that information because she was embarrassed by it. Apparently, while hypnotized, Catherine could censor some of the memories she transmitted back to me.

Since Catherine had recognized her niece in an ancient lifetime, I impulsively asked her if I was present in any of her lifetimes. I was curious about my role, if any, in her remembrances. She responded quickly, in contrast to the previous very slow and deliberate recall.

"You are my teacher, sitting on a ledge. You teach us from books. You are old with gray hair. You're wearing a white dress [toga] with gold trim. . . . Your name is Diogenes. You teach us symbols, triangles. You are very wise, but I don't understand. The year is 1568 B.C." (This was approximately twelve-hundred years before the noted Greek Cynic philosopher Diogenes. The name was not an uncommon one.)

The first session had ended. Even more amazing ones were yet to come.

After Catherine left, and over the next several days, I pondered the details of the hypnotic regression. It was natural for me to ponder. Very few details emerging from even a "normal" therapy hour escaped my obsessive mental analysis, and this session was hardly "normal." In addition, I was very skeptical about life after death, reincarnation, out-of-body experiences, and related phenomena. After all, the logical part of me ruminated, this could be her fantasy. I wouldn't actually be able to prove any of her assertions or visualizations. But I was also aware, although much more dimly, of a further and less emotional thought. Keep an open mind, the thought said; true science begins with observation. Her "memories" might *not* be fantasy or imagination. There might be something more than meets the eye—or any of the other senses. Keep an open mind. Get more data.

I had another nagging thought. Would Catherine, prone to anxieties and fears to begin with, be too frightened to undergo hypnosis again? I decided not to call her. Let her digest the experience, too. I would wait until next week.

Chapter
THREE

One week later, Catherine bounced into my office for her next hypnosis session. Beautiful to begin with, she was more radiant than ever. She happily announced that her lifelong fear of drowning had disappeared. Her fears of choking were somewhat diminished. Her sleep was no longer interrupted by the nightmare of a collapsing bridge. Although she had remembered the details of her past-life recall, she had not yet truly integrated the material.

The concepts of past lives and reincarnation were alien to her cosmology, and yet her memories were so vivid, the sights and sounds and smells so clear, the knowledge that she was there so powerful and immediate, that she felt she *must* have actually been there. She did not doubt this; the experience was so overwhelming. Yet she was concerned about how this fit in with her upbringing and her beliefs.

During the week I had reviewed my textbook from a comparative religions course taken during my freshman year at Columbia. There were indeed references to reincarnation in the Old and the New Testaments. In A.D. 325 the Roman emperor Constantine the Great, along with his mother, Helena, had deleted references to reincarnation contained in the New Testament. The Second Council of Constantinople, meeting in A.D. 553, confirmed this action and declared the concept of reincarnation a heresy. Apparently, they thought this concept would weaken the growing power of the Church by giving humans too much time to seek their salvation. Yet the original references had been there; the early Church fathers *had* accepted the concept of reincarnation. The early Gnostics—Clement of Alexandria, Origen, Saint Jerome, and many others—believed that they had lived before and would again.

I, however, had never believed in reincarnation. Actually, I had never really spent much time thinking about it. Although my earlier religious training taught about some kind of vague existence of the "soul" after death, I was not convinced about this concept.

I was the oldest of four children, all spaced three years apart. We belonged to a conservative Jewish synagogue in Red Bank, a small town near the New Jersey seashore. I was the peacemaker and statesman in my family. My father was more involved with religion than the rest of us were. He took it very seriously, as he took all of life. His children's academic achievements were the greatest joys in his life. He was easily upset by household discord and would withdraw, leaving me to mediate. Although this turned out to be excellent preparatory training for a career in psychiatry, my childhood was heavier and more responsible than, in retrospect, I would have preferred. I emerged from it as a very serious young man, one who got used to taking on too much responsibility.

My mother was always expressing her love. No boundary stood in her way. A simpler person than my father, she used guilt, martyrdom, terminal embarrassment, and vicarious identification with her children as manipulative tools, all without a second thought. Yet she was rarely gloomy, and we could always count on her love and support.

My father had a good job as an industrial photographer, and although we always had plenty of food, money was very tight. My youngest brother, Peter, was born when I was nine. We had to divide six people into our small two-bedroom garden apartment.

Life in this small apartment was hectic and noisy, and I sought refuge in my books. I read endlessly when not playing baseball or basketball, my other childhood passions. I knew that education was my path out of the small town, comfortable as it was, and I was always first or second in my class.

By the time I received a full scholarship to Columbia University, I was a serious and studious young man. Academic success continued to come easily. I majored in chemistry and was graduated with honors. I decided to become a psychiatrist because the field combined my interest in science and my fascination with the workings of the human mind. In addition, a career in medicine would allow me to express my concern and compassion for other people. In the meantime, I had met Carole during a summer vacation at a Catskill Mountain hotel where I was working as a busboy and she was a guest. We both experienced an immediate attraction to each other and a strong sense of familiarity and comfort. We corresponded, dated, fell in love, and were engaged by my junior year at Columbia. She was both bright and beautiful. Everything seemed to be falling into place. Few young men worry about life and death and life after death, especially when things are flowing smoothly, and I was no exception. I was becoming a scientist and learning to think in a logical, dispassionate, "prove-it" kind of way.

Medical school and residency at Yale University further

crystallized this scientific method. My research thesis was on brain chemistry and the role of neurotransmitters, which are chemical messengers in the brain tissue.

I joined the new breed of biological psychiatrists, those merging the traditional psychiatric theories and techniques with the new science of brain chemistry. I wrote many scientific papers, lectured at local and national conferences, and became quite a hotshot in my field. I was a bit obsessive, intense, and inflexible, but these were useful traits in a physician. I felt totally prepared to treat any person who walked into my office for therapy.

Then Catherine became Aronda, a young girl who had lived in 1863 B.C. Or was it the other way around? And here she was again, happier than I had ever seen her.

I again worried that Catherine might be afraid to continue. However, she eagerly prepared for the hypnosis and went under quickly.

"I am throwing wreaths of flowers on the water. This is a ceremony. My hair is blond and braided. I'm wearing a brown dress with gold, and sandals. Somebody has died, somebody in the Royal House . . . the mother. I am a servant with the Royal House, and I help with the food. We put the bodies in brine for thirty days. They dry out and the parts are taken out. I can smell it, smell the bodies."

She had spontaneously gone back to Aronda's lifetime, but to a different part of it, to when her duty was to prepare bodies after their death.

"In a separate building," Catherine continued, "I can see the bodies. We are wrapping bodies. The soul passes on. You take your belongings with you, to be prepared for the next and greater life." She was expressing what seemed like an Egyptian concept of death and the afterlife, different from any of our beliefs. In that religion, you *could* take it with you.

She left the lifetime and rested. She paused for several minutes before entering an apparently ancient time.

"I see ice, hanging in a cave . . . rocks. . . ." She vaguely described a dark and miserable place, and she was now visibly uncomfortable. Later she described what she had seen of herself. "I was ugly, dirty, and smelly." She left for another time.

"There are some buildings and a cart with stone wheels. My hair is brown with a cloth on it. The cart has straw in it. I'm happy. My father is there. . . . He's hugging me. It's . . . it's Edward [the pediatrician who insisted she see me]. He's my *father*. We live in a valley with trees. There are olive and fig trees in the yard. People write on papers. There are funny marks on them, like letters. People are writing all day, making a library. It is 1536 B.C. The land is barren. My father's name is Perseus."

The year did not fit exactly, but I was sure she was in the same lifetime that she had reported during the previous week's session. I took her ahead in time, staying in that lifetime.

"My father knows you [meaning me]. You and he talk about crops, law, and government. He says you are very smart and I should listen to you." I took her further ahead in time. "He's [father] lying in a dark room. He's old and sick. It's cold. . . . I feel so empty." She went ahead to her death. "Now I'm old and feeble. My daughter is there, near my bed. My husband is already dead. My daughter's husband is there, and their children. There are many people around."

Her death was peaceful this time. She was floating. Floating? This reminded me of Dr. Raymond Moody's studies of victims of near-death experiences. His subjects also remembered floating, then being pulled back to their bodies. I had read his book several years previously and now made a mental note to reread it. I wondered if Catherine could remember anything more after her death, but she could only say "I'm just floating." I awakened her and ended that session.

With a new insatiable hunger for any scientific papers that had been published on reincarnation, I hunted through the medical libraries. I studied the works of Ian Stevenson, M.D., a well-respected Professor of Psychiatry at the University of Virginia, who has published extensively in the psychiatric literature. Dr. Stevenson has collected over two thousand examples of children with reincarnation-type memories and experiences. Many exhibited xenoglossy, the ability to speak a foreign language to which they were never exposed. His case reports are carefully complete, well-researched, and truly remarkable.

I read an excellent scientific overview by Edgar Mitchell. With great interest I examined the ESP data from Duke University, and the writings of Professor C. J. Ducasse of Brown University, and I intently analyzed the studies of Dr. Martin Ebon, Dr. Helen Wambach, Dr. Gertrude Schmeidler, Dr. Frederick Lenz, and Dr. Edith Fiore. The more I read, the more I wanted to read. I began to realize that even though I had considered myself well educated about every dimension of the mind, my education had been very limited. There are libraries filled with this research and literature, and few people know about it. Much of this research was conducted, verified, and replicated by reputable clinicians and scientists. Could they all be mistaken or deceived? The evidence seemed to be overwhelmingly supportive, yet I still doubted. Overwhelming or not, I found it difficult to believe.

Both Catherine and I, in our own ways, had already been profoundly affected by the experience. Catherine was improving emotionally, and I was expanding the horizons of my mind. Catherine had been tormented by her fears for many years and was finally feeling some relief. Whether through actual memories or vivid fantasies, I had found a way to help her, and I was not going to stop now.

For a brief moment I thought about all of this as Catherine drifted into a trance at the beginning of the next session. Prior to the hypnotic induction, she had related a dream about a game being played on old stone steps, a game played with a checkerboard with holes in it. The dream had seemed especially vivid to her. I now told her to go back beyond the normal limits of space and time, to go back and see if her dream had roots in a previous reincarnation.

"I see steps leading up to a tower . . . overlooking the mountains, but also the sea. I am a boy. . . . My hair is blond . . . strange hair. My clothes are short, brown and white, made from animal skins. Some men are on top of the tower, looking out . . . guards. They are dirty. They play a game, like checkers, but not. The board is round, not square. They play with sharp, daggerlike pieces, which fit into the holes. The pieces have animal heads on them. Kirustan [phonetic spelling] Territory? From the Netherlands, around 1473."

I asked her the name of the place in which she lived, and whether she could see or hear a year. "I'm in a seaport now; the land goes down to the sea. There is a fortress . . . and water. I see a hut . . . my mother cooking in a clay pot. My name is Johan."

She was progressed to her death. At this point in our sessions, I was still looking for the single overwhelming traumatic event that could either cause or explain her current-life symptoms. Even if these remarkably explicit visualizations were fantasies, and I was unsure of this, what she believed or thought could still underlie her symptoms. After all, I had seen people traumatized by their dreams. Some could not remember whether a childhood trauma actually happened or oc-

curred in a dream, yet the memory of that trauma still haunted
their adult lives.

What I did not yet fully appreciate was that the steady
day-in and day-out pounding of undermining influences, such
as a parent's scathing criticisms, could cause even more psychological trauma than a single traumatic event. These dam-
aging influences, because they blend into the everyday background of our lives, are even more difficult to remember and
exorcise. A constantly criticized child can lose as much confidence and self-esteem as one who remembers being humili-
ated on one particular, horrifying day. A child whose family
is impoverished and has very little food available on a day-
to-day basis might eventually suffer from the same psychological problems as a child who experienced one major episode of
accidental near-starvation. I would soon realize that the day-in
and day-out pounding of negative forces had to be recognized
and resolved with as much attention as that paid to the single,
overwhelmingly traumatic event.

Catherine began to speak.

"There are boats, like canoes, brightly painted. Providence
area. We have weapons, spears, slings, bows and arrows, but
bigger. There are big, strange oars on the boat . . . everyone
has to row. We may be lost; it is dark. There are no lights.
I am afraid. There are other boats with us [apparently a raid-
ing party]. I'm afraid of the animals. We sleep on dirty, foul-
smelling animal skins. We are scouting. My shoes look funny,
like sacks . . . ties at the ankles . . . from animal skins.
[Long pause] My face is hot from the fire. My people are
killing the others, but I am not. I do not want to kill. My
knife is in my hand."

Suddenly she began to gurgle and gasp for breath. She reported that an enemy fighter had grabbed her from behind,
around the neck, and had slit her throat with his knife. She

saw the face of her killer before she died. It was Stuart. He looked different then, but she knew it was he. Johan had died at the age of twenty-one.

She next found herself floating above her body, observing the scene below. She drifted up to the clouds, feeling perplexed and confused. Soon she felt herself being pulled into a "tiny, warm" space. She was about to be born.

"Somebody is holding me," she whispered slowly and dreamily, "someone who helped with the birth. She's wearing a green dress with a white apron. She has a white hat, folded back at the corners. The room has funny windows . . . many sections. The building is stone. My mother has long, dark hair. She wants to hold me. There's a funny . . . rough nightshirt on my mother. It hurts to rub against it. It feels good to be in the sun and to be warm again. . . . It's . . . it's the *same* mother I have now!"

During the previous session, I had instructed her to closely observe the significant people in these lifetimes to see whether she could identify them as significant people in her present lifetime as Catherine. According to most writers, groups of souls tend to reincarnate together again and again, working out their karma (debts owed to others and to the self, lessons to be learned) over the span of many lifetimes.

In my attempt to understand this strange, spectacular drama that was unfolding, unbeknown to the rest of the world, in my quiet, dimly lighted office, I wanted to verify this information. I felt the need to apply the scientific method, which I had rigorously used over the past fifteen years in my research, to evaluate this most unusual material emerging from Catherine's lips.

Between sessions Catherine herself was becoming increasingly more psychic. She had intuitions about people and events that proved to be true. During the hypnosis, she had begun to anticipate my questions before I had a chance to ask them. Many of her dreams had a precognitive, or foretelling, bent.

On one occasion, when her parents came to visit her, her father expressed tremendous doubt about what was happening. To prove to him that it was true, she took him to the racetrack. There, right before his eyes, she proceeded to pick the winner of every race. He was stunned. Once she knew that she had proved her point, she took all of the money that she had won and gave it to the first poor streetperson she met on her way out of the track. She intuitively felt that the new spiritual powers she had gained should not be used for financial reward. For her, they had a much higher meaning. She told me that this experience was a little frightening to her, but she was so pleased with the progress she had made that she was eager to continue with the regressions. I was both shocked and fascinated by her psychic abilities, especially the episode at the racetrack. This was tangible proof. She had the winning ticket to every race. This was no coincidence. Something very odd was happening over these past several weeks, and I struggled to keep my perspective. I could not deny her psychic abilities. And if these abilities were real and could produce tangible proofs, could her recitations of past-life events also be true?

Now she returned to the lifetime in which she had just been born. This incarnation seemed to be more recent, but she could not identify a year. Her name was Elizabeth.

"I'm older now, with a brother and two sisters. I see the dinner table. . . . My father is there . . . he's Edward [the pediatrician, back for an encore performance as her father]. My mother and father are fighting again. The food is potatoes and beans. He's mad because the food is cold. They fight a lot. He's always drinking. . . . He hits my mother. [Catherine's voice was frightened, and she was trembling visibly.] He pushes the kids. He's not like he was before, not the same person. I don't like him. I wish he would go away." She was speaking as a child would speak.

My questioning of her during these sessions was certainly very different from what I used in conventional psychotherapy. I acted more as a guide with Catherine, trying to review an entire lifetime in an hour or two, searching for traumatic events and harmful patterns that might explain her current-day symptoms. Conventional therapy is conducted at a much more detailed and leisurely pace. Every word chosen by the patient is analyzed for nuances and hidden meanings. Every facial gesture, every bodily movement, every inflection of the voice is considered and evaluated. Every emotional reaction is carefully scrutinized. Behavior patterns are painstakingly pieced together. With Catherine, however, years could whir by in minutes. Catherine's sessions were like driving the Indy 500 at full throttle . . . and trying to pick out faces in the crowd.

I returned my attention to Catherine and asked her to advance in time.

"I'm married now. Our house has one big room. My husband has blond hair. I don't know him. [That is, he has not appeared in Catherine's present lifetime.] We have no children yet. . . . He's very nice to me. We love each other, and we're happy." Apparently she had successfully escaped from the oppression in her parental home. I asked if she could identify the area in which she lived.

"Brennington?" Catherine whispered hesitatingly. "I see books with funny old covers. The big one closes with a strap. It's the Bible. There are big fancy letters . . . Gaelic language."

Here she said some words I could not identify. Whether they were Gaelic or not, I have no idea.

"We live inland, not near the sea. County . . . Brennington? I see a farm with pigs and lambs. This is our farm." She had gone ahead in time. "We have two boys. . . . The older is getting married. I can see the church steeple . . . a very old stone building." Suddenly her head hurt, and Catherine was in pain, clutching her left temple area. She reported that she had fallen on the stone steps, but she recovered. She died of old age, in her bed at home with her family around.

She again floated out of her body after her death, but this time she was not perplexed or confused.

"I am aware of a bright light. It's wonderful; you get energy from this light." She was resting, after death, in between lifetimes. Minutes passed in silence. Suddenly she spoke, but not in the slow whisper she had always used previously. Her voice was now husky and loud, without hesitation.

"Our task is to learn, to become God-like through knowledge. We know so little. You are here to be my teacher. I have so much to learn. By knowledge we approach God, and then we can rest. Then we come back to teach and help others."

I was speechless. Here was a lesson from after her death, from the in-between state. What was the source of *this* material? This did not sound at all like Catherine. She had never spoken like this, using these words, this phraseology. Even the tone of her voice was totally different.

At that moment I did not realize that although Catherine had uttered the words, she had not originated the thoughts. She was relaying what was being said to her. She later identified the Masters, highly evolved souls not presently in body, as the source. They could speak to me through her. Not only could Catherine be regressed to past lifetimes, but now she could channel knowledge from the beyond. Beautiful knowledge. I struggled to retain my objectivity.

A new dimension had been introduced. Catherine had never read the studies of Dr. Elisabeth Kübler-Ross or Dr. Raymond Moody, who have both written about near-death experiences. She had never heard of the *Tibetan Book of the Dead*. Yet she was relating similar experiences to those described in these writings. This was a proof of sorts. If only there were more facts, more tangible details I could verify. My skepticism fluctuated, yet remained. Maybe she had read about near-death research in a magazine article or had seen an interview on a television show. Although she denied any conscious remembrance of such an article or show, perhaps she retained a subconscious memory. But she went beyond these previous writings and transmitted a message back from this in-between state. If only I had more facts.

After she awakened, Catherine remembered the details of her past lives, as always. However, she could not remember anything that happened after her death as Elizabeth. In the future she would never remember any details of the in-between states. She could only remember the lifetimes.

"By knowledge we approach God." We were on our way.

Chapter
FOUR

"I see a square white house with a sandy road in front. People on horses are going back and forth." Catherine was speaking in her usual dreamy whisper. "There are trees . . . a plantation, a big house with a bunch of smaller houses, like slave houses. It's very hot. It's in the South . . . Virginia?" She thought the date was 1873. She was a child.

"There are horses and lots of crops . . . corn, tobacco." She and the other servants ate in a kitchen of the big house. She was black, and her name was Abby. She felt a foreboding, and her body tensed. The main house was on fire, and she watched it burn down. I progressed her fifteen years in time to 1888.

"I'm wearing an old dress, cleaning a mirror on the second floor of a house, a brick house with windows . . . with lots of panes. The mirror is wavy, not straight, and it has knobs on the end. The man who owns the house is named James Manson. He has a funny coat with three buttons and a big black collar. He has a beard. . . . I don't recognize him [as someone in Catherine's present lifetime]. He treats me well. I live in a house on the property. I clean the rooms. There is a schoolhouse on the property, but I'm not allowed in the school. I make butter, too!"

Catherine was whispering slowly, using very simple terms

and paying great attention to detail. Over the next five minutes, I learned how to make butter. Abby's knowledge of churning butter was new to Catherine, too. I moved her ahead in time.

"I am with somebody, but I don't think we are married. We sleep together . . . but we don't always live together. I feel okay about him, but nothing special. I don't see any children. There are apple trees and ducks. Other people are in the distance. I'm picking apples. Something is making my eyes itch." Catherine was grimacing with her eyes closed. "It's the smoke. The wind is blowing it this way . . . the smoke from burning wood. They're burning up wooden barrels." She was coughing now. "It happens a lot. They're making the inside of the barrels black . . . tar . . . to waterproof."

After the excitement of last week's session, I was eager to reach the in-between state again. We had already spent ninety minutes exploring her lifetime as a servant. I had learned about bedspreads, butter, and barrels; I was hungry for a more spiritual lesson. Forsaking my patience, I advanced her to her death.

"It's hard to breathe. My chest hurts so much." Catherine was gasping, in obvious pain. "My heart hurts; it's beating fast. I'm so cold . . . my body's shaking." Catherine began to shiver. "People are in the room, giving me leaves to drink [a tea]. It smells funny. They're rubbing a liniment on my chest. Fever . . . but I feel very cold." She quietly died. Floating up to the ceiling, she could see her body in the bed, a small, shriveled woman in her sixties. She was just floating, waiting for someone to come and help her. She became aware of a light, feeling herself drawn toward it. The light was becoming brighter, and more luminous. We waited in silence as minutes slowly passed. Suddenly she was in another lifetime, thousands of years before Abby.

Catherine was softly whispering, "I see lots of garlic, hanging in an open room. I can *smell* it. It is believed to kill many evils in the blood and to cleanse the body, but you must take it every day. The garlic is outside too, on top of a garden. Other herbs are there . . . figs, dates, and other herbs. These plants help you. My mother is buying garlic and the other herbs. Somebody in the house is sick. These are strange roots. Sometimes you just keep them in your mouth, or ears, or other openings. You just keep them in.

"I see an old man with a beard. He's one of the healers in the village. He tells you what to do. There is some type of . . . plague . . . killing the people. They're not embalming because they're afraid of the disease. People are just buried. The people are unhappy about this. They feel the soul cannot pass on this way [contrary to Catherine's after-death reports]. But so many have died. The cattle are dying, too. Water . . . floods . . . people are sick because of the floods. [She apparently just realized this bit of epidemiology.] I also have some disease from the water. It makes your stomach hurt. The disease is of the bowel and stomach. You lose so much water from the body. I'm by the water to bring more back, but that's what is killing us. I bring the water back. I see my mother and brothers. My father has already died. My brothers are very sick."

I paused before progressing her in time. I was fascinated by the way her conceptions of death and the afterlife changed so much from lifetime to lifetime. And yet her *experience* of death itself was so uniform, so similar, every time. A conscious part of her would leave the body around the moment of death, floating above and then being drawn to a wonderful, energizing light. She would then wait for someone to come and help her. The soul automatically passed on. Embalming, burial rituals, or any other procedure after death had nothing to do with it. It was automatic, no preparation necessary, like walking through a just-opened door.

"The land is barren and dry. . . . I see no mountains around here, just land, very flat and dry. One of my brothers has died. I'm feeling better, but the pain is still there." However, she did not live much longer. "I'm lying on a pallet with some type of covering." She was very ill, and no amount of garlic or other herbs could prevent her death. Soon she was floating above her body, drawn to the familiar light. She waited patiently for someone to come to her.

Her head began to roll slowly from side to side, as if she were scanning some scene. Her voice was again husky and loud.

"They tell me there are many gods, for God is in each of us."

I recognized the voice from the in-between–lives state by its huskiness as well as by the decidedly spiritual tone of the message. What she said next left me breathless, pulling the air from my lungs.

"Your father is here, and your son, who is a small child. Your father says you will know him because his name is Avrom, and your daughter is named after him. Also, his death was due to his heart. Your son's heart was also important, for it was backward, like a chicken's. He made a great sacrifice for you out of his love. His soul is very advanced. . . . His death satisfied his parents' debts. Also he wanted to show you that medicine could only go so far, that its scope is very limited."

Catherine stopped speaking, and I sat in an awed silence as my numbed mind tried to sort things out. The room felt icy cold.

Catherine knew very little about my personal life. On my

desk I had a baby picture of my daughter, grinning happily with her two bottom baby teeth in an otherwise empty mouth. My son's picture was next to it. Otherwise Catherine knew virtually nothing about my family or my personal history. I had been well schooled in traditional psychotherapeutic techniques. The therapist was supposed to be a tabula rasa, a blank tablet upon which the patient could project her own feelings, thoughts, and attitudes. These then could be analyzed by the therapist, enlarging the arena of the patient's mind. I had kept this therapeutic distance with Catherine. She really knew me only as a psychiatrist, nothing of my past or of my private life. I had never even displayed my diplomas in the office.

The greatest tragedy in my life had been the unexpected death of our firstborn son, Adam, who was only twenty-three days old when he died, early in 1971. About ten days after we had brought him home from the hospital, he had developed respiratory problems and projectile vomiting. The diagnosis was extremely difficult to make. "Total anomalous pulmonary venous drainage with an atrial septal defect," we were told. "It occurs once in approximately every ten million births." The pulmonary veins, which were supposed to bring oxygenated blood back to the heart, were incorrectly routed, entering the heart on the wrong side. It was as if his heart were turned around, *backward*. Extremely, extremely rare.

Heroic open-heart surgery could not save Adam, who died several days later. We mourned for months, our hopes and dreams dashed. Our son, Jordan, was born a year later, a grateful balm for our wounds.

At the time of Adam's death, I had been wavering about my earlier choice of psychiatry as a career. I was enjoying my internship in internal medicine, and I had been offered a residency position in medicine. After Adam's death, I firmly decided that I would make psychiatry my profession. I was angry that modern medicine, with all of its advanced skills and technology, could not save my son, this simple, tiny baby.

My father had been in excellent health until he experienced a massive heart attack early in 1979, at the age of sixty-one. He survived the initial attack, but his heart wall had been irretrievably damaged, and he died three days later. This was about nine months before Catherine's first appointment.

My father had been a religious man, more ritualistic than spiritual. His Hebrew name, Avrom, suited him better than the English, Alvin. Four months after his death, our daughter, Amy, was born, and she was named after him.

Here, in 1982, in my quiet, darkened office, a deafening cascade of hidden, secret truths was pouring upon me. I was swimming in a spiritual sea, and I loved the water. My arms were gooseflesh. Catherine could not possibly know this information. There was no place even to look it up. My father's *Hebrew* name, that I had a son who died in infancy from a one-in-ten million heart defect, my brooding about medicine, my father's death, and my daughter's naming—it was too much, too specific, too true. This unsophisticated laboratory technician was a conduit for transcendental knowledge. And if she could reveal these truths, what else was there? I needed to know more.

"Who," I sputtered, "who is there? Who tells you these things?"

"The Masters," she whispered, "the Master Spirits tell me. They tell me I have lived eighty-six times in physical state."

Catherine's breathing slowed, and her head stopped rolling from side to side. She was resting. I wanted to go on, but the implications of what she had said were distracting me. Did she really have eighty-six previous lifetimes? And what about "the Masters"? Could it be? Could our lives be guided by spirits who have no physical bodies but who seem to possess great knowledge. Are there steps on the way to God? Was this real? I found it difficult to doubt, in view of what she had just revealed, yet I still struggled to believe. I was overcoming years of alternative programming. But in my head and my heart and my gut, I knew she was right. She was revealing truths.

And what about my father and my son? In a sense, they were still alive; they had never really died. They were talking to me, years after their burials, and proving it by providing specific, very secret information. And since all that was true, was my son as advanced spiritually as Catherine had said? Did he indeed agree to be born to us and then die twenty-three days later in order to help us with our karmic debts and, in addition, to teach me about medicine and humankind, to nudge me back to psychiatry? I was very heartened by these thoughts. Beneath my chill, I felt a great love stirring, a strong feeling of oneness and connection with the heavens and the earth. I had missed my father and my son. It was good to hear from them again.

My life would never be the same again. A hand had reached down and irreversibly altered the course of my life. All of my reading, which had been done with careful scrutiny and skeptical detachment, fell into place. Catherine's memories and messages were true. My intuitions about the accuracy of her experiences had been correct. I had the facts. I had the proof.

Yet, even in that very instant of joy and understanding, even in that moment of the mystical experience, the old and familiar logical and doubting part of my mind lodged an objection. Perhaps it's just ESP or some psychic skill. Granted, it's quite a skill, but it doesn't prove reincarnation or Master Spirits. Yet this time I knew better. The thousands of cases recorded in the scientific literature, especially those of children speaking foreign languages to which they had never been exposed, of having birthmarks at the site of previous mortal wounds, of these same children knowing where treasured objects were hidden or buried thousands of miles away and decades or centuries earlier, all echoed Catherine's message. I knew Catherine's character and her mind. I knew what she was and what she wasn't. No, my mind could not fool me this time. The proof was too strong and too overwhelming. This was real. She would verify more and more as our sessions progressed.

At times over the succeeding weeks I would forget the power and immediacy of this session. At times I would fall back into the rut of everyday life, worrying about the usual things. Doubts would surface. It was as if my mind, when not focused, tended to drift back into the old patterns, beliefs, and skepticism. But then I would remind myself—this actually happened! I appreciated how difficult it is to believe these concepts without having personal experience. The experience is necessary to add emotional belief to intellectual understanding. But the impact of experience always fades to some degree.

At first, I was not aware of why I was changing so much. I knew I was more calm and patient, and others were telling me how peaceful I looked, how I seemed more rested and happier. I felt more hope, more joy, more purpose, and more satisfaction in my life. It dawned on me that I was losing the fear of death. I wasn't afraid of my own death or of nonexistence. I was less afraid of losing others, even though I would certainly miss them. How powerful the fear of death is. People go to such great lengths to avoid the fear: mid-life crises, affairs with younger people, cosmetic surgeries, exercise obsessions, accumulating material possessions, procreating to carry on a name, striving to be more and more youthful, and so on.

We are frightfully concerned with our own deaths, sometimes so much so that we forget the real purpose of our lives.

I was also becoming less obsessive. I didn't need to be in control all the time. Although I was trying to become less serious, this transformation was difficult for me. I still had much to learn.

My mind was indeed now open to the possibility, even the probability, that Catherine's utterances were real. The incredible facts about my father and my son could not be obtained through the usual senses. Her knowledge and abilities certainly proved an outstanding psychic ability. It made sense to believe her, but I remained wary and skeptical about what I read in the popular literature. Who are these people reporting psychic phenomena, life after death, and other amazing paranormal events? Are they trained in the scientific method of observation and validation? Despite my overwhelming and wonderful experience with Catherine, I knew my naturally critical mind would continue to scrutinize every new fact, every piece of information. I would check to see if it fit into the framework being built with every session. I would examine it from every angle, with a scientist's microscope. And yet I could no longer deny that the framework was already there.

Chapter
FIVE

We were still in the middle of the session. Catherine ended her rest and began talking about green statues in front of a temple. I roused myself from my reverie and listened. She was in an ancient lifetime, somewhere in Asia, but I was still with the Masters. Incredible, I thought to myself. She's talking about previous lifetimes, about *reincarnation,* and yet compared to hearing messages from the Masters, it feels anticlimactic. I was already realizing, however, that she had to go through a lifetime before she could leave her body and reach the in-between state. She could not reach this state directly. And it was only there that she could reach the Masters.

"The green statues are in front of a large temple building," she whispered softly, "a building with peaks and brown balls. There are seventeen steps in front, and there is a room after you climb the steps. Incense is burning. Nobody has shoes. Their heads are shaven. They have round faces and dark eyes. They are dark skinned. I am there. I have hurt my foot and have gone there for help. My foot is swollen; I can't step on it. Something is stuck in my foot. They put some leaves on my foot . . . strange leaves . . . Tannis? [Tannin, or tannic acid, which occurs naturally in the roots, wood, bark, leaves, and fruit of many plants, has been used since ancient times as a medicine because of its styptic or astringent properties.] First my foot was cleansed. This is a ritual before the gods. There is some poison in my foot. I stepped on something. My knee is swollen. My leg is heavy with streaks on it [blood poisoning?]. They cut a hole in the foot and put something very hot on it."

Catherine was now writhing in pain. She was also gagging from some terribly bitter potion that she was given to drink. The potion was made from yellow leaves. She healed, but the bones in her foot and her leg were never the same again. I progressed her in time. She saw only a bleak and poverty-stricken life. She lived with her family in a small one-room hut without a table. They ate some kind of rice, like a cereal, but they were always hungry. She aged rapidly, never escaping the poverty or the hunger, and she died. I waited, but I could see Catherine's exhaustion. Before I could awaken her, however, she told me that Robert Jarrod needed my help. I had no idea who Robert Jarrod was, or how I could help him. There was no more.

After awakening from the trance, Catherine again remembered many of the details of her past-life recall. She remembered nothing at all of the after-death experiences, nothing from the in-between state, nothing of the Masters or of the incredible knowledge that had been revealed. I asked her a question.

"Catherine, what does the term 'Masters' mean to you?" She thought this was a golf tournament! She was improving rapidly now, but she still had difficulty integrating the concept of reincarnation into her theology. Therefore, I decided not to tell her about the Masters yet. Besides, I wasn't sure how you broke the news to someone that she was an incredibly talented trance medium who could channel wonderful, transcendental knowledge from the Master Spirits.

Catherine agreed to allow my wife to attend the next session. Carole is a well-trained, highly skilled psychiatric social worker, and I wanted her opinion about these incredible happenings. After I told her what Catherine had said about my father and our son, Adam, she was eager to help. I had no trouble taking notes of every word from the lifetimes when Catherine whispered quite slowly, but the Masters spoke much more quickly, and I decided to tape-record everything.

One week later Catherine came in for her next session. She continued to improve, with diminished fears and anxieties. Her clinical improvement was definite, but I still was not sure why she was so much better. She had remembered drowning as Aronda, having her throat slashed as Johan, being a victim of a water-borne epidemic as Louisa, and other terrifyingly traumatic events. She had also experienced or re-experienced lifetimes of poverty and servitude and of abuse within her family. The latter are examples of the day-in and day-out minitraumas that also get ground into our psyches. The remembrance of both types of lifetimes could be contributing to her improvement. But another possibility existed. Could the spiritual experience itself be helping? Could the knowledge that death is not what it appears to be contribute to a sense of well-being, of diminution of fears? Could the entire *process*, not just the memories themselves, be part of the cure?

Catherine's psychic abilities were increasing, and she was becoming even more intuitive. She still had problems with Stuart, but she felt able to cope with him more effectively. Her eyes sparkled; her skin glowed. She had had a strange dream during the week, she announced, but she could only remember a fragment of it. She had dreamed that the red fin of a fish was embedded in her hand.

She went under quickly and easily, reaching a deep level of hypnosis within minutes.

"I see some type of cliffs. I'm standing on the cliffs, looking down. I should be looking for ships—that's what I'm supposed to be doing. . . . I'm wearing something blue, a blue type of pants . . . short pants with strange shoes . . . black shoes . . . and they buckle. The shoes have buckles, very funny shoes. . . . I see on the horizon there are no ships." Catherine was whispering softly. I progressed her in time to the next significant event in her life.

"We're drinking ale, stout ale. It's very dark. The tankards are thick. They're old, put together with metal stays. It's very foul-smelling in this place, and many people are in there. It's very loud. Everybody is talking, very noisy."

I asked her if she could hear anybody calling her name.

"Christian . . . Christian is my name." She was a male again. "We're just eating some type of meat and drinking ale. It's dark and very bitter-tasting. They put salt on it."

She could not see a year. "They're talking about a war, about ships blockading some ports! But I can't hear where it is. If they would be quiet, we could hear, but everyone's talking and noisy."

I asked her where she was. "Hamstead . . . Hamstead [phonetic spelling]. It's a port, a seaport in Wales. They're talking British." She went ahead in time to when Christian was on his ship. "I can *smell* something, something burning. It's a terrible smell. Burning wood, but also something else. It burns your nose. . . . Something in the distance is on fire, some type of vessel, a sailing vessel. We're loading! We're loading something with gunpowder." Catherine was becoming visibly agitated.

"It's something with gunpowder, very black. It sticks to your hands. You have to move fast. The ship has a green flag on it. The flag is dark. . . . It's a green and yellow flag. There is some type of crown with three points on it."

Suddenly Catherine grimaced with pain. She was in agony. "Uh," she grunted, "the pain in my hand, the pain in my hand!

There's some metal, hot metal in my hand. It's burning me! Oh! Oh!"

I remembered the dream fragment and understood now about the red fin embedded in her hand. I blocked the pain, but she was still moaning.

"The splinters are metal. . . . The ship we were on was destroyed . . . the port side. They have the fire under control. Many men have been killed . . . many men. I have survived . . . only my hand is hurt, but it heals with time." I took her ahead in time, letting her pick out the next significant event.

"I see some type of printshop, printing something with blocks and ink. They're printing and binding books. . . . The books have leather covers and strings holding them together, leather strings. I see a red book. . . . It's something about history. I can't see the title; they haven't finished the printing. The books are wonderful. Their covers are so smooth, the leather. They're wonderful books; they teach you."

Obviously Christian enjoyed seeing and touching the books, and he dimly realized the potential of learning this way. He seemed to be largely uneducated, however. I progressed Christian to the last day of his life.

"I see a bridge over a river. I'm an old man . . . very old. It's difficult to walk. I'm walking over the bridge . . . to the other side. . . . I feel pain in my chest—pressure, terrible pressure—pain in my chest! Oh!" Catherine was making gurgling sounds, experiencing the apparent heart attack that Christian was having on the bridge. Her breathing was rapid and shallow; her face and neck were covered with sweat. She began to cough and to gasp for air. I was concerned. Was reexperiencing a heart attack from a previous lifetime dangerous? This was a new frontier; nobody knew the answers. Finally, Christian died. Catherine was now lying peacefully on the couch, breathing deeply and evenly. I let out a deep sigh of relief.

"I feel free . . . free," Catherine gently whispered. "I'm just floating in darkness . . . just floating. There is a light around . . . and spirits, other people."

I asked if she had any thoughts about the lifetime that had just ended, her life as Christian.

"I should have been more forgiving, but I wasn't. I did not forgive the wrongs that people did to me, and I should have. I didn't forgive the wrongs. I held them inside, and I harbored them for many years. . . . I see eyes . . . eyes."

"Eyes?" I echoed, sensing the contact. "What kind of eyes?"

"The eyes of the Master Spirits," Catherine whispered, "but I must wait. I have things to think about." Minutes passed in tense silence.

"How will you know when they are ready," I asked expectantly, breaking the long silence.

"They will call me," she answered. More minutes passed. Then, suddenly, her head began to roll from side to side, and her voice, hoarse and firm, signaled the change.

"There are many souls in this dimension. I am not the only one. We must be patient. That is something I never learned either. . . . There are many dimensions. . . ." I asked her whether she had been here before, whether she had reincarnated many times.

"I have been to different planes at different times. Each one is a level of higher consciousness. What plane we go to depends upon how far we've progressed. . . ." She was silent again. I asked her what lessons she had to learn in order to progress. She answered immediately.

"That we must share our knowledge with other people. That we all have abilities far beyond what we use. Some of us find this out sooner than others. That you should check your vices before you come to this point. If you do not, you carry them over with you to another life. Only we can rid ourselves . . . of the bad habits that we accumulate when we are in a physical state. The Masters cannot do that for us. If you choose to fight and not to rid yourself, then you will carry them over into another life. And only when you decide that you are strong enough to master the external problems, then you will no longer have them in your next life.

"We also must learn not to just go to those people whose vibrations are the same as ours. It is normal to feel drawn to somebody who is on the same level that you are. But this is wrong. You must also go to those people whose vibrations are wrong . . . with yours. This is the importance . . . in helping . . . these people.

"We are given intuitive powers we should follow and not try to resist. Those who resist will meet with danger. We are not sent back from each plane with equal powers. Some of us possess powers greater than others, because they have been accrued from other times. Thus people are not all created equal. But eventually we will reach a point where we will all be equal."

Catherine paused. I knew these thoughts were not hers. She had no background in physics or metaphysics; she knew nothing about planes and dimensions and vibrations. But beyond that, the beauty of the words and thoughts, the philosophical implications of these utterings—these were all beyond Catherine's capabilities. She had never talked in such a concise, poetic manner. I could feel another, higher force struggling with her mind and vocal cords to translate these thoughts into words, so that I could understand. No, this was not Catherine.

Her voice had a dreamy tone.

"People who are in comas . . . are in a state of suspension. They are not ready yet to cross into the other plane . . . until they have decided whether they want to cross or not. Only they can decide this. If they feel they have no more learning . . . in physical state . . . then they are allowed to cross over. But if they have more learning, then they must come back, even if they do not want to. That is a rest period for them, a time when their mental powers can rest."

So people in comas can decide whether or not to return, depending upon how much learning they have yet to accomplish in the physical state. If they feel there is nothing further to learn, they can go directly to the spiritual state, modern medicine notwithstanding. This information meshed nicely with the research being published about near-death experiences, and why some people chose to return. Others were not given the choice; they had to return because there was more to learn. Of course, all of the people interviewed about their near-death experiences returned to their bodies. There is a striking similarity in their stories. They become detached from their bodies and "watch" resuscitation efforts from a point above their bodies. They eventually become aware of a bright light or a glowing "spiritual" figure in the distance, sometimes at the end of a tunnel. They feel no pain. As they become aware that their tasks on earth are not yet completed, and they must return to their bodies, they are immediately rejoined to their bodies and once again are aware of pain and other physical sensations.

I have had several patients with near-death experiences. The most interesting account was that of a successful South American businessman who was seen by me for several sessions of conventional psychotherapy about two years after Catherine's treatment ended. Jacob had been run over and knocked unconscious by a motorcycle in Holland in 1975, when he was in his early thirties. He remembers floating above his body and looking down at the scene of the accident, taking note of the ambulance, the doctor attending his injuries, and the growing crowd of onlookers. He became aware of a golden light in the distance, and as he approached it, he saw a monk wearing a brown robe. The monk told Jacob that this was not his time to pass over, that he had to return to his body. Jacob felt the wisdom and power of the monk, who also related several future events in Jacob's life, all of which later occurred. Jacob was whooshed back into his body, now in a hospital bed, regained consciousness, and, for the first time, became aware of excruciating pain.

In 1980, while traveling in Israel, Jacob, who is Jewish, visited the Cave of the Patriarchs in Hebron, which is a holy site to both Jews and Muslims. After his experience in Holland, he had become more religious and had begun to pray more often. He saw the nearby mosque and sat down to pray with the Muslims there. After a while, he rose to leave. An old Muslim man came up to him and said, "You are different from the others. They very rarely sit down to pray with us." The old man paused for a moment, looking closely at Jacob before continuing. "You have met the monk. Do not forget what he has told you." Five years after the accident and thousands of miles distant, an old man knew about Jacob's encounter with the monk, an encounter that happened while Jacob had been unconscious.

In the office, pondering Catherine's latest revelations, I wondered what our Founding Fathers would have thought about the proposition that all humans are not created equal. People are born with talents, abilities, and powers accrued from other lifetimes. "But eventually we will reach a point where we will all be equal." I suspected that this point was many, many lifetimes distant.

I thought about the young Mozart and his incredible child-hood talents. Was this also a carry-over of former abilities? Apparently we carried over abilities as well as debts.

I thought about how people tended to congregate in homogeneous groups, avoiding and often fearing outsiders. This was the root of prejudice and group hatreds. "We also must learn not to just go to those people whose vibrations are the same as ours." To *help* these other people. I could feel the spiritual truths in her words.

"I must come back," Catherine resumed. "I must come back." But I wanted to hear more. I asked her who Robert Jarrod was. She had mentioned his name during the last session, stating that he needed my help.

"I don't know. . . . He may be in another plane, not this one." Apparently she could not find him. "Only when he wants, only if he decides to come to me," she whispered, "he will send me a message. He needs your help."

I still could not understand how I could help.

"I don't know," Catherine answered. "But you are the one to be taught, not I."

This was interesting. Was this material for me? Or was I to help Robert Jarrod by being taught? We never did hear from him.

"I must go back," she repeated. "I must go to the light first." Suddenly she was alarmed. "Oh, oh, I've hesitated much too long. . . . Because I hesitated I have to wait again." While she waited, I asked her what she was seeing and feeling.

"Just other spirits, other souls. They're waiting, too." I asked her whether there was something to teach us while she was waiting. "Can you tell us what we must know?" I asked.

"They are not here to tell me," she replied. Fascinating. If the Masters were not there for her to hear, Catherine could not independently provide the knowledge.

"I'm very restless being here. I do want to go. . . . When the time is right, I will go." Again, minutes silently passed. Finally the time must have been right. She had fallen into another lifetime.

"I see apple trees . . . and a house, a white house. I live in the house. The apples are rotten . . . worms, no good to eat. There is a swing, a swing on the tree." I asked her to look at herself.

"I have light hair, blond hair; I'm five years old. My name is Catherine." I was surprised. She had entered her present lifetime; she was Catherine at age five. But she must be there for some reason. "Did something happen there, Catherine?"

"My father is angry at us . . . 'cause we're not supposed to be outside. He . . . he's hitting me with a stick. It's very heavy; it hurts. . . . I'm afraid." She was whining, speaking like a child. "He won't stop till he's hurt us. Why does he do this to us? Why is he so mean?" I asked her to see her life from a higher perspective and to answer her own questions. I had recently read about people being able to do this. Some writers called this perspective one's Higher Self or Greater Self. I was curious whether Catherine could reach this state, if it existed. If she could, this would be a powerful therapeutic technique, a shortcut to insight and understanding.

"He never wanted us," she whispered very softly. "He feels we're an intrusion in his life. . . . He doesn't want us."

"Your brother, too?" I asked.

"Yes, my brother even more. They never planned for my brother. They weren't married when . . . he was conceived." This proved to be startling new information for Catherine. She had never known about the premarital pregnancy. Her mother later confirmed the accuracy of Catherine's revelation.

Although she was recounting a lifetime, Catherine now exhibited a wisdom and a perspective about her life that had previously been restricted to the in-between, or spiritual, state. Somehow there was a "higher" part of her mind, a sort of superconscious. Perhaps this was the Higher Self that others have described. Although not in contact with the Masters and their spectacular knowledge, nevertheless, in her superconscious state she possessed profound insights and information, such as her brother's conception. The conscious Catherine, when awake, was much more anxious and limited, much simpler and comparatively superficial. She could not tap into this superconscious state. I wondered if the prophets and sages of Eastern and Western religions, those called "actualized," were able to utilize this superconscious state to obtain their wisdom and knowledge. If so, then we all had the ability to do so, for we must all possess this superconscious. The psychoanalyst Carl Jung was aware of the different levels of consciousness. He wrote about the collective unconscious, a state with similarities to Catherine's superconscious.

I would become increasingly frustrated by the uncrossable gulf between Catherine's conscious, awake intellect and her trance-level superconscious mind. While she was hypnotized, I would have fascinating philosophical dialogues with her at the superconscious level. When awake, however, Catherine had no interest in philosophy or related matters. She lived in the world of everyday detail, oblivious of the genius within her.

Meanwhile, her father was tormenting her, and the reasons were becoming evident. "He has many lessons to learn," I stated in a questioning way.

"Yes . . . so he does."

I asked her if she knew what he had to learn. "This knowledge is not revealed to me." Her tone was detached, distant. "What is revealed to me is what is important to me, what concerns me. Each person must be concerned with him- or herself . . . with making him- or herself . . . whole. We have lessons to learn . . . each one of us. They must be learned one at a time . . . in order. Only then can we know what the next person needs, what he or she lacks or what we lack, to make us whole." She spoke in a soft whisper, and her whisper conveyed a feeling of loving detachment.

When Catherine spoke again, the childlike voice had returned. "He's making me sick! He's making me eat this stuff that I don't want. It's some food . . . lettuce, onions, stuff I hate. He's making me eat it, and he knows I'm gonna be sick. But he doesn't care!" Catherine began to gag. She was gasping for air. I again suggested that she view the scene from a higher perspective, that she needed to understand why her father acted this way.

Catherine spoke in a raspy whisper. "It must fill some void in him. He hates me because of what he did. He hates me for that, and he hates himself." I had nearly forgotten about the sexual assault when she was three years old. "So he must punish me. . . . I must have done something to make him do that." She was only three years old, and her father was drunk. Yet she had carried this guilt deep within her ever since. I explained the obvious.

"You were just a baby. You must now relieve yourself of this guilt. You didn't do anything. What could a three-year-old do? It wasn't you; it was your father."

"He must have hated me then, too," she gently whispered. "I knew him before, but I cannot draw on that information now. I must go back to that time." Although several hours had already passed, I wanted to go back to their previous relationship. I gave her detailed instructions.

"You are in a deep state. In a moment I am going to count

backward, from three to one. You will be in a deeper state and will feel totally safe. Your mind will be free to roam back in time again, back to the time when the connection to your father in your current life began, back to the time that had the most significant bearing on what happened in your childhood between you and him. When I say 'one,' you will go back to that lifetime and remember it. It is important for your cure. You can do that. Three . . . two . . . one." There was a long pause.

"I do not see him . . . but I see people being killed!" Her voice became loud and husky. "We have no right to abruptly halt peoples' lives before they have lived out their karma. And we are doing it. We have no right. They will suffer greater retribution if we let them live. When they die and go to the next dimension, they will suffer there. They will be left in a very restless state. They will have no peace. And they will be sent back, but their lives will be very hard. And they will have to make up to those people that they hurt for the injustices that they did against them. They are halting these people's lives, and they have no right to do that. Only God can punish them, not us. They will be punished."

A minute of silence passed. "They are gone," she whispered. The Master Spirits had given us one more message today, strong and clear. We are not to kill, no matter what the circumstances. Only God can punish.

Catherine was exhausted. I decided to postpone our pursuit of the past-life connection to her father, and I brought her out of her trance. She remembered nothing except her incarnations as Christian and as young Catherine. She was tired, yet peaceful and relaxed, as if a huge weight had been lifted from her. My eyes met Carole's. We were also exhausted. We had shivered and we had sweated, hanging on to every word. We had shared an incredible experience.

Chapter
SIX

I now scheduled Catherine's weekly sessions at the end of the day, because they were lasting several hours. She still had that peaceful look about her when she came in the following week. She had talked with her father on the phone. Without giving him any details, she had, in her way, forgiven him. I had never seen her this serene. I marveled at the rapidity of her progress It was rare for a patient with such chronic, deep-seated anxieties and fears to improve so dramatically. But then, of course, Catherine was hardly an ordinary patient, and the course her therapy had taken was certainly unique.

"I see a porcelain doll sitting on some type of mantel." She had quickly fallen into a deep trance. "There are books next to the fireplace on both sides. It's a room within some house. There are candlesticks next to the doll. And a painting . . . of the face, the man's face. It's him. . . ." She was scanning the room. I asked her what she was seeing.

"Some type of covering on the floor. It's fuzzy like it's . . . it is an animal skin, yes . . . some type of animal-skin covering on the floor. To the right there are two glass doors . . . that lead out onto the veranda. There are four steps—columns on the front of the house—four steps down. They lead out to a path. Big trees are all around. . . . There are some horses outside. The horses are bridled . . . to some posts that are sitting out front."

"Do you know where this is?" I inquired. Catherine took a deep breath.

"I don't see a name," she whispered, "but the year, the year must be somewhere. It's the eighteenth century, but I don't . . . there are trees and yellow flowers, very pretty yellow flowers." She was distracted by these flowers. "They smell wonderful; they smell sweet, the flowers . . . strange flowers, big flowers . . . yellow flowers with black centers in them." She paused, remaining among the flowers. I was reminded of a field of sunflowers in the south of France. I asked her about the climate.

"It's very temperate, but it's not breezy. It's neither hot nor cold." We were not making any progress in identifying the locale. I took her back into the house, away from the fascinating yellow flowers, and I asked her whose portrait was above the mantel.

"I can't . . . I keep hearing Aaron . . . his name is Aaron." I asked if he owned the house. "No, his son does. I work there." Once again she was cast as a servant. She had never even remotely approached the status of a Cleopatra or a Napoleon. Doubters of reincarnation, including my own scientifically trained self until the past two months, often point to the much higher than expected frequency of incarnations as famous people. Now I found myself in the most unusual position of having reincarnation being proved scientifically right in my offices in the Department of Psychiatry. And much more than reincarnation was being revealed.

"My leg is very . . ." Catherine continued, "very heavy. It hurts. It almost feels like it's not there. . . . My leg is hurt. The horses kicked me." I told her to look at herself.

"I have brown hair, brown curly hair. I have some type of

bonnet on, some type of white bonnet . . . a blue dress with some type of pinafore on the dress . . apron. I'm young, but not a child. But my leg hurts. It just happened. It hurts terribly." She was visibly in great pain. "Shoe . . . shoe. He kicked me with his shoe. He's a very, very mean horse." Her voice grew softer as the pain finally subsided. "I can smell the hay, the feed in the barn. There are other people working in the stable area." I asked about her duties.

"I was responsible for serving . . . for serving in the big house. I also had something to do with milking the cows." I wanted to know more about the owners.

"The wife is rather plump, very dowdy-looking. And there are two daughters. . . . I do not know them," she added, anticipating my next question whether any had appeared yet in Catherine's current lifetime. I inquired about her own family in the eighteenth century.

"I don't know; I don't see them. I don't see anybody with me." I asked if she lives there. "I lived here, yes, but not in the main house. Very small . . . the house is provided for us. There are chickens. We gather up the eggs. They're brown eggs. My house is very small . . . and white . . . one room. I see a man. I live with him. He has very curly hair and blue eyes." I asked if they are married.

"Not their understanding of marriage, no." Was she born there? "No, I was brought to the estate when I was very young. My family was very poor." Her mate did not seem familiar. I directed her to move ahead in time to the next significant event in that lifetime.

"I see something white . . . white with many ribbons on it. Must be a hat. Some type of bonnet, with feathers and white ribbons."

"Who is wearing the hat? Is it—" She cut me off.

"The lady of the house, of course." I felt a bit stupid. "It's the marriage of one of their daughters. The whole estate joined in the celebration." I asked if there was anything in the newspaper about the wedding. If there was, I would have had her look at the date.

"No, I don't believe they have newspapers there. I see nothing like that." Documentation was proving difficult to come by in this lifetime. "Do you see yourself at the wedding?" I asked. She answered quickly, in a loud whisper.

"We're not at the wedding. We can only watch the people coming and going. The servants are not allowed."

"What are you feeling?"

"Hatred."

"Why? Do they treat you poorly?"

"Because we are poor," she answered softly, "and we're bonded to them. And we have so little compared to what they have."

"Do you ever get to leave the estate? Or do you live out your life there?"

She answered wistfully. "I live out my life there." I could feel her sadness. Her life was both difficult and hopeless. I progressed her to the day of her death.

"I see a house. I'm lying in bed, lying on the bed. They're giving me something to drink, something warm. It has a minty odor to it. My chest is very heavy. It's difficult to breathe. . . . I have pain in my chest and my back. . . . It's a bad pain . . . difficult to talk." She was breathing rapidly and shallowly, in great pain. After a few minutes of agony, her face softened, and her body relaxed. Her breathing returned to normal.

"I have left my body." Her voice was louder and husky. "I see a wonderful light. . . . There are people coming to me. They are coming to help me. Wonderful people. They are not afraid. . . . I feel very light. . . ." There was a long pause.

"Do you have any thoughts about the lifetime you just left?"

"That is for later. For now, I just feel the peace. It's a time of comfort. The party must be comforted. The soul . . . the soul finds peace here. You leave all the bodily pains behind you. Your soul is peaceful and serene. It's a wonderful feeling . . . wonderful, like the sun is always shining on you. The light is so brilliant! Everything comes from the light! Energy comes from this light. Our soul *immediately* goes there. It's almost like a magnetic force that we're attracted to. It's wonderful. It's like a power source. It knows how to heal."

"Does it have a color?"

"It's many colors." She paused, resting in this light.

"What are you experiencing?" I ventured.

"Nothing . . . just peacefulness. You're among your friends. They are all there. I see many people. Some are familiar; others are not. But we're there, waiting." She continued to wait, as minutes slowly passed. I decided to push the pace.

"I have a question to ask."

"Of whom," Catherine asked.

"Somebody—you or the Masters," I hedged. "I think the understanding of this will help us. The question is this: Do we choose the times and the manner of our birth and our death? Can we choose our situation? Can we choose the time of our passing over again? I think understanding that will ease a lot of your fears. Is there anyone there who can answer that question?" The room felt cold. When Catherine spoke again, her voice was deeper and more resonant. It was a voice I had never heard before. It was the voice of a poet.

"Yes, we choose when we will come into our physical state and when we will leave. We know when we have accomplished what we were sent down here to accomplish. We know when the time is up, and you will accept your death.

For you know that you can get nothing more out of this lifetime. When you have time, when you have had the time to rest and re-energize your soul, you are allowed to choose your re-entry back into the physical state. Those people who hesitate, who are not sure of their return here, they might lose the chance that was given them, a chance to fulfill what they must when they're in physical state."

I knew immediately and completely that this was not Catherine speaking. "Who is speaking to me," I implored; "who is talking?"

Catherine answered in her familiar soft whisper. "I don't know. The voice of someone very . . . somebody who controls things, but I don't know who it is. I can only hear his voice and try to tell you what he says."

She also knew this knowledge was not coming from herself, not from the subconscious, nor from the unconscious. Not even her superconscious self. She was somehow listening to, then conveying to me, the words or thoughts of someone very special, someone who "controls things." Thus another Master had appeared, different from the one, or several, from whom the previous wisdom-laden messages had come. This was a new spirit, with a characteristic voice and style, poetic and serene. This was a Master who spoke about death without any hesitation, yet whose voice and thoughts were steeped with love. The love felt warm and real, yet detached and universal. It felt blissful, yet not smothering or emotional or binding. It relayed a feeling of loving detachment or detached loving-kindness, and it felt distantly familiar.

Catherine's whisper grew louder. "I have no faith in these people."

"No faith in which people?" I queried.

"In the Masters."

"No faith?"

"No, I have lack of faith. That's why my life has been so difficult. I had no faith in that lifetime." She was calmly evaluating her eighteenth-century life. I asked her what she had learned in that lifetime.

"I learned about anger and resentment, about harboring your feelings toward people. I also had to learn that I have no control over my life. I want control, but I don't have any. I must have faith in the Masters. They will guide me throughout. But I did not have the faith. I felt like I was doomed from the beginning. I never looked at things very pleasantly. We must have faith . . . we must have faith. And I doubt. I choose to doubt instead of believe." She paused.

"What should you do, and I do, to make ourselves better? Are our paths the same?" I asked. The answer came from the Master who last week had spoken of intuitive powers and of returning from comas. The voice, the style, the tone, were all different from both Catherine's and from the masculine, poetic Master who had just spoken.

"Everybody's path is basically the same. We all must learn certain attitudes while we're in physical state. Some of us are quicker to accept them than others. Charity, hope, faith, love . . . we must all know these things and know them well. It's not just one hope and one faith and one love—so many things feed into each one of these. There are so many ways to demonstrate them. And yet we've only tapped into a little bit of each one. . . .

"People of the religious orders have come closer than any of us have because they've taken these vows of chastity and obedience. They've given up so much without asking for anything in return. The rest of us continue to ask for rewards— rewards and justifications for our behavior . . . when there are no rewards, rewards that *we* want. The reward is in doing, but doing without expecting anything . . . doing unselfishly.

"I have not learned that," Catherine added, in her soft whisper.

For a moment I was confused by the word "chastity," but I remembered that the root meant "pure," referring to a much different state from that of just sexual abstinence.

". . . Not to overindulge," she continued. "Anything done to excess . . . in excess. . . . You will understand. You really *do* understand." She paused again.

"I'm trying," I added. Then I decided to focus on Catherine. Perhaps the Masters had not yet left. "What can I do to best help Catherine to overcome her fears and anxieties? And to learn her lessons? Is this the best way, or should I change something? Or follow up in a specific area? How can I help her the best?"

The answer came in the deep voice of the poet Master. I leaned forward in my chair.

"You are doing what is correct. But this is for you, not for her." Once again, the message was that this was for my benefit more than for Catherine's.

"For me?"

"Yes. What we say is for you." Not only was he referring to Catherine in the third person, but he said "we." There were, indeed, several Master Spirits in attendance.

"Can I know your names?" I asked, immediately wincing at the mundane nature of my question. "I need guidance. I have so much to know."

The answer was a love poem, a poem about my life and my death. The voice was soft and tender, and I felt the loving detachment of a universal spirit. I listened in awe.

"You will be guided in time. You will be guided . . . in time. When you accomplish what you have been sent here to accomplish, then your life will be ended. But not before then. You have much time ahead of you . . . much time."

I was simultaneously anxious and relieved. I was glad he was not more specific. Catherine was becoming restless. She spoke in a small whisper.

"I'm falling, falling . . . trying to find my life . . . falling." She sighed, and I did, too. The Masters were gone. I pondered the miraculous messages, very personalized messages from very spiritual sources. The implications were overwhelming. The light after death and the life after death; our choosing when we are born and when we will die; the sure and unerring guidance of the Masters; lifetimes measured in lessons learned and tasks fulfilled, not in years; charity, hope, faith, and love; doing without expectations of return—this knowledge was for me. But for what purpose? What *was* I sent here to accomplish?

The dramatic messages and events cascading upon me in the office mirrored deep changes in my personal and family life. The transformation gradually crept into my awareness. For example, I was driving with my son to a college baseball game when we became stuck in a huge traffic jam. I have always been annoyed by traffic jams, and now we would miss the first inning or two as well. I was aware of not being annoyed. I wasn't projecting the blame on some incompetent driver. My neck and shoulder muscles were relaxed. I didn't take out my irritation on my son, and we were passing the time talking to each other. I became aware of just wanting to spend a happy afternoon with Jordan, watching a game we both enjoy. The goal of the afternoon was to spend time together. If I had become annoyed and angry, the whole outing would have been ruined.

I would look at my children and my wife and wonder if we had been together before. Had we chosen to share the trials and tragedies and joys of this life? Were we ageless? I felt a great love and tenderness toward them. I realized that their flaws and faults are minor. These are not really so important. Love is.

I even found myself overlooking my own flaws, for the same reasons. I didn't need to try to be perfect or in control all the time. There really was no need to impress anyone.

I was very glad that I could share this experience with Carole. We would often talk after dinner and sort out my feelings and reactions to Catherine's sessions. Carole has an analytical mind and is very well grounded. She knew how driven I was to pursue the experience with Catherine in a careful, scientific manner, and she would play the devil's advocate to help me look at this information objectively. As the critical evidence mounted that Catherine was indeed revealing great truths, Carole felt and shared my apprehensions and my joys.

Chapter
SEVEN

When Catherine arrived for her next appointment one week later, I was ready to play the tape of last week's incredible dialogue. After all, she was providing me with celestial poetry in addition to past-life recall. I told her that she had related information from after-death experiences, even though she had no memory at all of the in-between or spiritual state. She was reluctant to listen. Overwhelmingly improved and happier, she had no need to listen to this material. Besides, it was all somewhat "eerie." I prevailed upon her to listen. It was wonderful, beautiful, uplifting, and it came through her. I wanted to share it with her. She listened to her soft whisper on the tape for only a few minutes, and then she made me turn it off. She said that it was just too weird and made her uncomfortable. Silently, I remembered "this is for you, not for her."

I wondered how long these sessions would continue because she was improving every week. Now only a few ripples remained in her once-turbulent pond. She was still afraid of enclosed places, and the relationship with Stuart was still literally touch and go. Otherwise her progress was remarkable.

We had not had a traditional psychotherapy session for months. None was necessary. We would chat for a few minutes to catch up on the events of the week, then move quickly to the hypnotic regression. Whether due to the actual memories of major traumas or daily minitraumas or to the process of reliving the experiences, Catherine was virtually cured. Her phobias and panic attacks had just about disappeared. She had no fear of death or dying. She was no longer afraid of losing control. Psychiatrists are now using high doses of tranquilizers and antidepressant medicines to treat people with Catherine's symptoms. In addition to the medicines, the patients are also often in intensive psychotherapy or attending phobia group therapy sessions. Many psychiatrists believe that symptoms such as Catherine's have a biological basis, that there are deficiencies in one or several brain chemicals.

As I hypnotized Catherine to a deep trance state, I thought about how remarkable and wonderful it was that in a period of weeks, without the use of medicines, traditional therapy, or group therapy, she was nearly cured. This was not just the suppression of symptoms nor the gritting of teeth and living through it, a life racked by fears. This was a cure, the absence of symptoms. And she was radiant, serene, and happy beyond my wildest hopes.

Her voice was a soft whisper again. "I'm in a building, something with a domed ceiling. The ceiling is blue and gold. There are other people with me. They're dressed in . . . old . . . some type of robe, very old and dirty. I don't know how we got there. There are many figures in the room. There are also some pieces, some pieces standing on some stone structure. There's a large gold figure at one end of the room. He appears. . . . He's very large, with wings. He's very evil. It's very hot in the room, very hot. . . . It's hot because there are no openings into the room. We have to stay away from the village. There's something wrong with us."

"Are you sick?"

"Yes, we are all sick. I don't know what it is we have, but

our skin dies. It becomes very black. I feel very cold. The air is very dry, very stale. We cannot return to the village. We must stay out. Some of the faces are deformed."

This disease sounded terrible, like leprosy. If she had once had a glamorous lifetime, we had not yet stumbled across it. "How long do you have to stay there?"

"Forever," she answered gloomily, "until we die. There is no cure for this."

"Do you know the name of the illness? What is it called?"

"No. The skin gets very dry and shrivels up. I have been there for years. There are others who have just arrived. There is no way back. We have been cast out . . . to die."

She suffered a wretched existence, living in a cave.

"We must hunt for our food. I see some type of wild beast that we are hunting for . . . with horns. He's brown with horns, big horns."

"Does anybody visit you?"

"No, they cannot go near or they will suffer from the evil, too. We have been cursed . . . for some evil we have done. And this is our punishment." The sands of her theology were constantly shifting in the hourglass of her lives. Only after death, in the spiritual state, was there a welcome and reassuring constancy.

"Do you know what year it is?"

"We have lost track of time. We are sick; we just await our death."

"Is there no hope?" I felt the infectious despair.

"There is no hope. We will all die. And there is much pain in my hands. My whole body is weak. I am old. It is difficult for me to move."

"What happens when you cannot move anymore?"

"You are moved to another cave, and you're left there to die."

"What do they do with the dead?"

"They seal the entrance to the cave."

"Do they ever seal a cave before the person is dead?" I was searching for a clue to her fear of enclosed places.

"I do not know. I have never been there. I'm in the room with other people. It's very hot. I'm against the wall, just lying there."

"What is the room for?"

"It is for the worship . . . many gods. It's very hot."

I advanced her in time. "I see something white. I see something white, some type of canopy. They're moving somebody."

"Is it you?"

"I don't know. I will welcome death. My body is in so much pain." Catherine's lips were drawn thin in pain, and she was panting because of the heat in the cave. I took her to the day of her death. She was still panting.

"Is it hard to breathe?" I asked.

"Yes, so hot in here . . . feels . . . so hot, very dark. I can't see . . . and I can't move." She was dying, paralyzed and alone, in the hot, dark cave. The mouth of the cave was already sealed shut. She was frightened and miserable. Her breathing grew more rapid and irregular, and she mercifully died, ending this anguished life.

"I feel very light . . . like I'm floating. It's very bright here. It's wonderful!"

"Are you in pain?"

"No!" She paused, and I awaited the Masters. Instead, she was whisked away. "I'm falling very fast. I'm going back to a body!" She seemed as surprised as I was.

"I see buildings, buildings with round columns. There are many buildings. We are outside. There are trees—olive trees— around. It's very beautiful. We are watching something. . . .

People have on very funny masks; these cover their faces. It is some festivities. They're dressed in long robes, and they have masks that cover their faces. They pretend to be what they're not. They are on a platform . . . above where we sit."

"Are you watching a play?"

"Yes."

"What do you look like? Look at yourself."

"I have brown hair. My hair is in a braid." She paused. Her description of herself and the presence of olive trees reminded me of Catherine's Greek-like lifetime fifteen hundred years before Christ, when I was her teacher, Diogenes. I decided to investigate.

"Do you know the date?"

"No."

"Are there people with you that you know?"

"Yes, my husband is sitting next to me. I do not know him" [in her present lifetime].

"Do you have children?"

"I am with child now." Her choice of words was interesting, somehow ancient and not at all like Catherine's conscious style.

"Is your father there?"

"I do not see him. You are there somewhere . . . but not with me." So I was right. We were back thirty-five centuries.

"What do I do there?"

"You are just watching, but you teach. You teach. . . . We have learned from you . . . squares and circles, funny things. Diogenes, you are there."

"What else do you know of me?"

"You are old. Somehow we are related . . . you are my mother's brother."

"Do you know others of my family?"

"I know your wife . . . and your children. You have sons. Two of them are older than I. My mother has died; she died very young."

"Has your father raised you?"

"Yes, but I am married now."

"You're expecting a baby?"

"Yes. I'm afraid. I do not want to die while the baby is born."

"Did that happen to your mother?"

"Yes."

"And you're afraid it will happen to you also?"

"It happens many times."

"Is this your first child?"

"Yes; I am frightened. I expect it soon. I'm very big. It is uncomfortable for me to move. . . . It is cold." She had moved herself ahead in time. The baby was about to be born. Catherine had never had a baby, and I had not delivered any in the fourteen years since my obstetrics rotation in medical school.

"Where are you?" I inquired.

"I'm lying on something stone. It's very cold. I'm having pain. . . . Somebody must help me. Somebody *must* help me." I told her to breathe deeply; the baby would be born without pain. She was panting and groaning at the same time. Her labor lasted several more agonizing minutes, and then her child was born. She had a daughter.

"Do you feel better now?"

"Very weak . . . so much blood!"

"Do you know what you will name her?"

"No, I'm too tired. . . . I want my baby."

"Your baby is here," I ad-libbed, "a little girl."

"Yes, my husband is pleased." She was exhausted. I instructed her to take a short nap and to awaken refreshed. After a minute or two, I awakened her from the nap.

"Do you feel better now?"

"Yes. . . . I see animals. They are carrying something on their backs. They have baskets on them. There are many things in the baskets . . . food . . . some red fruits. . . ."

"Is it a pretty land?"

"Yes, with much food."

"Do you know the name of the land? What do you call it when a stranger asks you the name of the village?"

"Cathenia . . . Cathenia."

"It sounds like a Greek town," I prompted.

"I don't know that. Do you know that? You have been away from the village and returned. I have not." This was a twist. Since, in that lifetime, I was her uncle, older and wiser, she was asking me if I knew the answer to my own question. Unfortunately, I did not have access to that information.

"Have you lived all your life in the village?" I asked.

"Yes," she whispered, "but you travel, so you can know what you teach. You travel to learn, to learn the land . . . the different trade routes so you can put them down and make maps. . . . You are old. You go with the younger people because you understand the charts. You are very wise."

"Which charts do you mean? Charts of the stars?"

"You, you understand the symbols. You can help them to make . . . help them to make maps."

"Do you recognize other people from the village?"

"I do not know them . . . but I know you."

"All right. How is our relationship?"

"Very good. You are very kind. I like to just sit next to you; it's very comforting. . . . You have helped us. You have helped my sisters. . . ."

"There comes a time, though, when I must leave you, for I am old."

"No." She was not ready to deal with my death. "I see some bread, flat bread, very flat and thin."

"Are people eating the bread?"

"Yes, my father and my husband and I. And other people in the village."

"What is the occasion?"

"It is some . . . some festival."

"Is your father there?"

"Yes."

"Is your baby there?"

"Yes, but she's not with me. She's with my sister."

"Look closely at your sister," I suggested, looking for that recognition of a significant person in Catherine's current life.

"Yes. I do not know her."

"Do you recognize your father?"

"Yes . . . yes . . . Edward. There are figs, figs and olives . . . and red fruit. There is flat bread. And they have killed some sheep. They are roasting the sheep." There was a long pause. "I see something white. . . ." She had again progressed herself in time. "It's a white . . . it's a square box. It's where they put people when they die."

"Did someone die, then?"

"Yes . . . my father. I don't like to look at him. I don't want to see him."

"Do you have to look?"

"Yes. They will take him away to bury him. I feel very sad."

"Yes, I know. How many children do you have?" The reporter in me was not letting her grieve.

"I have three, two boys and a girl." After dutifully answering my question, she returned to her grief. "They have put his body under something, under some cover. . . ." She seemed very sad.

"Have I died by this time, too?"

"No. We are drinking some grapes, grapes in a cup."

"What do I look like now?"

"You are very, very old."

"Are you feeling better yet?"

"No! When you die I'll be alone."

"Have you outlived your children? They will take care of you."

"But you know so much." She sounded like a little girl.

"You will get by. You know a lot, too. You'll be safe." I reassured her, and she appeared to be resting peacefully.

"Are you more peaceful? Where are you now?"

"I don't know." She had apparently crossed over into the spiritual state, even though she had not experienced her death in that lifetime. This week we had gone through two lifetimes in considerable detail. I awaited the Masters, but Catherine continued to rest. After several more minutes of waiting, I asked if she could talk to the Master Spirits.

"I have not reached that plane," she explained. "I cannot speak until I do."

She never did reach that plane. After much waiting, I brought her out of the trance.

Chapter
EIGHT

Three weeks passed before our next session. On my vacation, lying on a tropical beach, I had the time and distance to reflect on what had transpired with Catherine: hypnotic regression to past lives with detailed observations and explanations of objects, processes, and facts—which she had no knowledge of in her normal, waking state; improvement in her symptoms through the regressions—improvement not even remotely achieved by conventional psychotherapy over the first eighteen months of treatment; chillingly accurate revelations from the after-death, spiritual state, conveying knowledge she had no access to; spiritual poetry, and lessons about the dimensions after death, about life and death, birth and rebirth, from Master Spirits who spoke with a wisdom and in a style well beyond Catherine's capabilities. There was, indeed, a lot to contemplate.

Over the years I had treated many hundreds, perhaps thousands, of psychiatric patients, and they reflected the entire spectrum of emotional disorders. I had directed inpatient units at four major medical schools. I had spent years in psychiatric emergency rooms, outpatient clinics, and various other settings, evaluating and treating outpatients. I knew all about the auditory and visual hallucinations and the delusions of schizophrenia. I had treated many patients with borderline syndromes and hysterical character disorders, including split or multiple personalities. I had been a Career Teacher in Drug and Alcohol Abuse, funded by the National Institute of Drug Abuse (NIDA), and I was very familiar with the gamut of drug effects on the brain.

Catherine had none of these symptoms or syndromes. What had occurred was not a manifestation of psychiatric illness. She was not psychotic, not out of touch with reality, and she had never suffered from hallucinations (seeing or hearing things not actually there) or delusions (false beliefs).

She did not use drugs, and she had no sociopathic traits. She did not have a hysterical personality, and she did not have dissociative tendencies. That is, she was generally aware of what she was doing and thinking, did not function on "automatic pilot," and had never had any split or multiple personalities. The material she produced was often beyond her conscious capabilities in both style and content. Some of it was particularly psychic, such as the references to specific events and facts from my own past (e.g., the knowledge about my father and my son), as well as from her own. She had knowledge that she had never had access to, or accumulated, in her present life. This knowledge, as well as the whole experience, was alien to her culture and upbringing and contrary to many of her beliefs.

Catherine is a relatively simple and honest person. She is not a scholar, and she could not have invented the facts, details, historical events, descriptions, and poetry that came through her. As a psychiatrist, a scientist, I was certain that the material originated from some portion of her unconscious mind. It was real, beyond any doubt. Even if Catherine were a skilled actress, she could not have recreated these happenings. The knowledge was too accurate and too specific, lying beyond her capacity.

I pondered the therapeutic purpose of exploring Catherine's past lives. Once we had stumbled into this new realm, her improvement was dramatically rapid, without any medicine. There is some powerful curative force in this realm, a force apparently much more effective than conventional therapy or modern medicines. The force includes remembering and re-living not just momentous traumatic events, but also the daily insults to our bodies, minds, and egos. In my questions, as we scanned lifetimes, I was looking for the patterns of these in-sults, patterns such as chronic emotional or physical abuse, poverty and starvation, illness and handicaps, persistent per-secution and prejudice, repeated failures, and so on. I also kept an eye out for those more piercing tragedies, such as a trau-matic death experience, rape, mass catastrophe, or any other horrifying event that might leave a permanent imprint. The technique was similar to reviewing a childhood in conventional therapy, except that the time frame was several *thousand* years, rather than the usual ten or fifteen years. Therefore my ques-tions were more direct and more leading than in conventional therapy. But the success of our unorthodox exploration was unquestionable. She [and others I later would treat with hyp-notic regression] was being cured with tremendous rapidity.

But were there other explanations for Catherine's past-life memories? Could the memories be carried in her genes? This possibility is scientifically remote. Genetic memory requires the unbroken passage of genetic material from generation to generation. Catherine lived all over the earth, and her genetic line was interrupted repeatedly. She would die in a flood with her offspring, or be childless, or die in her youth. Her genetic pool ended and was not transmitted. And what of her survival after death and the in-between state? There was no body and certainly no genetic material, and yet her memories continued. No, the genetic explanation had to be discarded.

What about Jung's idea of the collective unconscious, a reservoir of all human memory and experience that could somehow be tapped into? Divergent cultures often contain similar symbols, even in dreams. According to Jung, the collective unconscious was not personally acquired but "inherited" somehow in the brain structure. It includes motives and images that spring anew in every culture, without relying upon historical tradition or dissemination. I thought Catherine's memories were too specific to be explained by Jung's concept. She did not reveal symbols and universal images or motives. She related detailed descriptions of specific people and places. Jung's ideas seemed too vague. And there was still the in-between state to consider. All in all, reincarnation made the most sense.

Catherine's knowledge was not only detailed and specific, but also beyond her conscious capacity. She knew things that could not be gleaned from a book and then temporarily forgotten. Her knowledge could not have been acquired in her childhood and then similarly suppressed or repressed from consciousness. And what about the Masters and their messages? This came through Catherine but was not of Catherine. And their wisdom was also reflected in Catherine's memories of lifetimes. I knew that this information and these messages were true. I knew this not only from many years of careful study of people, their minds and brains and personalities, but I also knew this intuitively, even before the visit from my father and my son. My brain with its years of careful scientific training knew this, and my bones also knew.

"I see pots with some type of oil in them." Despite the three-week hiatus, Catherine had quickly lapsed into a deep trance. She was enmeshed in another body, in another time. "There are different oils in the pots. It seems to be some type of storehouse or someplace where they store things. The pots are red . . . red, made out of some type of red earth. They have blue bands around them, blue bands around the top. I see men there . . . there are men in the cave. They're moving the jars and the pots around, stacking them up and putting them in a certain area. Their heads are shaved . . . they have no hair on their heads. Their skin is brown . . . brown skin."

"Are you there?"

"Yes . . . I'm sealing up some of the jars . . . with some type of wax . . . sealing the top of the jars with the wax."

"Do you know what the oils are used for?"

"I don't know."

"Do you see yourself? Look at yourself. Tell me what you look like." She paused as she observed herself.

"I have a braid. There's a braid in my hair. I have some type of long . . . long-material garment on. It has a gold border around the outside."

"Do you work for these priests—or the men—with the shaved heads?"

"It is my job to seal the jars with the wax. That's my job."

"But you don't know what the jars are used for?"

"They appear to be used in some religious ritual. But I'm not sure . . . what it is. There's some anointing, something on the heads . . . something on your heads and your hands, your hands. I see a bird, a gold bird, that's around my neck. It's flat. It has a flat tail, a very flat tail, and its head is pointing down . . . to my feet."

"To your feet?"

"Yes, that's the way it must be worn. There's a black . . . black sticky substance. I don't know what it is."

"Where is it?"

"It's in a marble container. They use that, too, but I don't know what for."

"Is there anything in the cave for you to read so that you can tell me the name of the country—the place—where you live, or the date?"

"There's nothing on the walls; they're empty. I do not know the name." I progressed her in time.

"There's a white jar, some type of white jar. The handle on the top is gold, some type of gold inlay on it."

"What is in the jar?"

"Some type of ointment. It has something to do with the passage into the other world."

"Are you the person to be passing now?"

"No! It is no one I know."

"Is this your job, too? To prepare people for this passage?"

"No. The priest must do that, not me. We just keep them supplied with the ointments, the incense. . . ."

"About how old do you appear to be now?"

"Sixteen."

"Are you living with your parents?"

"Yes, a stone house, some type of stone dwelling. It's not very large. It's very hot and dry. The climate is very hot."

"Go to your house."

"I'm there."

"Do you see other people around in your family?"

"I see a brother, and my mother is there, and a baby, somebody's baby."

"Is that your baby?"

"No."

"What is significant now? Go to something significant that explains your symptoms in your current lifetime. We need to understand. It is safe to experience it. Go to the events."

She answered in a very soft whisper. "Everything in time. . . . I see people dying."

"People dying?"

"Yes . . . they don't know what it is."

"An illness?" Suddenly it dawned on me that she was again touching on an ancient lifetime, one that she had regressed to previously. In that lifetime, a water-borne plague had killed Catherine's father and one of her brothers. Catherine had also suffered from the illness, but she had not died from it. The people used garlic and other herbs to try to ward off the plague. Catherine had been upset because the dead were not being properly embalmed.

But now we had approached that lifetime from a different angle. "Does it have something to do with the water?" I asked.

"They believe so. Many people are dying." I already knew the ending.

"But you don't die, not from this?"

"No, I do not die."

"But you get sick. You become ill."

"Yes, I'm very cold . . . very cold. I need water . . . water. They think it comes from the water . . . and something black. . . . Someone dies."

"Who dies?"

"My father dies, and one brother dies also. My mother is okay; she recovers. She's very weak. They must bury the people. They must bury them, and people are upset because it's against religious practices."

"What was the practice?" I marveled at the consistency of her recall, fact for fact, exactly as she had recounted the lifetime several months ago. Again this deviation from the normal burial customs greatly upset her.

"People were put in caves. The bodies were kept in caves. But first, the bodies had to be prepared by the priests. They must be wrapped and anointed. They were kept in caves, but the land is flooding. . . . They say the water is bad. Don't drink the water."

"Is there a way of treating it? Did anything work?"

"We were given herbs, different herbs. The odors . . . the herbs and . . . smell the odor. I can smell it!"

"Do you recognize the smell?"

"It's white. They hang it from the ceiling."

"Is it like garlic?"

"It's hung around . . . the properties are similar, yes. Its properties . . . you put it in your mouth, your ears, your nose, everywhere. The odor was strong. It was believed to block the evil spirits from entering your body. Purple . . . fruit or something round with purple covering, purple skin to it. . . ."

"Do you recognize the culture that you're in? Does it seem familiar?"

"I don't know."

"Is the purple a fruit of some sort?"

"Tannis."

"Would that help you? Is that for the illness?"

"It was at that time."

"Tannis," I repeated, again trying to see if she was talking about what we refer to as tannin or tannic acid. "Is that what they called it? Tannis?"

"I just . . . I keep hearing 'Tannis.' "

"What in this lifetime has buried itself in your current lifetime? Why do you keep coming back here? What is it that is so uncomfortable?"

"The religion," Catherine quickly whispered, "the religion of that time. It was a religion of fear . . . fear. There were so many things to fear . . . and so many gods."

"Do you remember the names of any gods?"

"I see eyes. I see a black . . . some type of . . . it looks like a jackal. He's in a statue. He's a guardian of some type . . . I see a woman, a goddess, with some type of a head-piece on."

"Do you know her name, the goddess?"

"Osiris . . . Sirus . . . something like that. I see an eye . . . eye, just an eye, an eye on a chain. It's gold."

"An eye?"

"Yes. . . . Who is Hathor?"

"What?"

"Hathor! Who is that!"

I had never heard of Hathor, although I knew that Osiris, if the pronunciation was accurate, was the brother-husband of Isis, a major Egyptian deity. Hathor, I later learned, was the Egyptian goddess of love, mirth, and joy. "Is it one of the gods?" I asked.

"Hathor! Hathor." There was a long pause "Bird . . . he's flat . . . flat, a phoenix. . . ." She was silent again.

"Go ahead in time now to your final day in that lifetime. Go to your final day, but before you have died. Tell me what you see."

She answered in a very soft whisper. "I see people and buildings. I see sandals, sandals. There is a rough cloth, some type of rough cloth."

"What happens? Go to the time of your dying now. What happens to you? You can see it."

"I do not see it . . . I don't see *me* anymore."

"Where are you? What do you see?"

"Nothing . . . just darkness. . . . I see a light, a warm light." She had already died, already passed over to the spiritual state. Apparently she did not need to experience her actual death again.

"Can you come to the light?" I asked.

"I am going." She was resting peacefully, waiting again.

"Can you look backward now on the lessons of that lifetime? Are you aware of them yet?"

"No," she whispered. She continued to wait. Suddenly she appeared alert, although her eyes remained closed, as they always did when she was in hypnotic trances. Her head was turning from side to side.

"What are you seeing now? What's happening?"

Her voice was louder. "I feel . . . someone's talking to me!"

"What do they say?"

"Talking about patience. One must have patience. . . ."

"Yes, go on."

The answer came from the poet Master. "Patience and timing . . . everything comes when it must come. A life cannot be rushed, cannot be worked on a schedule as so many people want it to be. We must accept what comes to us at a given time, and not ask for more. But life is endless, so we never die; we were never really born. We just pass through different phases. There is no end. Humans have many dimensions. But time is not as we see time, but rather in lessons that are learned."

There was a long pause. The poet Master continued.

"Everything will be clear to you in time. But you must have a chance to digest the knowledge that we have given to you already." Catherine was silent.

"Is there more I should learn?" I asked.

"They've gone," she softly whispered. "I don't hear anybody."

Chapter
NINE

Each week another layer of neurotic fears and anxieties was stripped away from Catherine. Each week she appeared a bit more serene, a bit softer and more patient. She was more confident, and people were drawn to her. Catherine felt more loving, and others gave love back to her. The inner diamond that was her true personality was shining brilliantly for all to see.

Catherine's regressions spanned millennia. Each time she entered a hypnotic trance, I had no idea where the threads of her lives would emerge. From prehistoric caves to ancient Egypt to modern times—she had been there. And all of her lives had been lovingly overseen, somewhere beyond time, by the Masters. In today's session she emerged in the twentieth century, but not as Catherine.

"I see a fuselage and an airstrip, some kind of airstrip," she whispered softly.

"Do you know where it is?"

"I can't see . . . Alsatian?" Then, more definitely, "Alsatian."

"In France?"

"I don't know, just Alsatian. . . . I see the name Von Marks, Von Marks [phonetic]. Some type of brown helmet or a hat . . . a hat with goggles on it. The troop has been destroyed. It appears to be a very remote area. I don't think there's a town nearby."

"What do you see?"

"I see buildings destroyed. I see buildings. . . . The land is torn up from . . . bombings. There's a very well hidden area."

"What are you doing?"

"I'm helping them with the wounded. They're carrying them away."

"Look at yourself. Describe yourself. Look down and see what you're wearing."

"I have some type of jacket on. I have blond hair. I have blue eyes. My jacket is very dirty. There are many wounded people."

"Are you trained to help with the wounded?"

"No."

"Do you live there or were you brought there? Where do you live?"

"I don't know."

"About how old are you?"

"Thirty-five." Catherine herself was twenty-nine, and she had hazel eyes, not blue. I continued the questioning.

"Do you have a name? Is it on the jacket?"

"There are wings on the jacket. I'm a pilot . . . some type of pilot."

"You fly the airplanes?"

"Yes, I have to."

"Who makes you fly?"

"I'm in service to fly. That's my job."

"Do you drop the bombs, too?"

"We have a gunner on the plane. There's a navigator."

"What kind of plane do you fly?"

"Some type of chopper plane. It has four propellers. It's a fixed wing." I was amused, because Catherine knew nothing about airplanes. I wondered what she would think "fixed wing" meant. But, like the making of butter or the embalming of the deceased, under hypnosis she possessed a vast store of knowledge. Only a fraction of this knowledge, however, was available to her everyday, conscious mind. I pressed on.

"Do you have a family?"

"They are not with me."

"Are they safe?"

"I don't know. I'm afraid . . . afraid they will come back. My friends are dying!"

"Who are you afraid will come back?"

"The enemy."

"Who are they?"

"The English . . . the American Armed Forces . . . the English."

"Yes. Do you remember your family?"

"Remember it? There's too much confusion."

"Let's go back in the same lifetime, back to a happier time, before the war, the time with your family back at home. You can see that. I know it's hard, but I want you to relax. Try and remember."

Catherine paused, then whispered, "I hear the name Eric . . . Eric. I see a blond-haired child, a girl."

"Is that your daughter?"

"Yes, it must be . . . Margot."

"Is she close to you?"

"She's with me. We're on a picnic. The day is beautiful."

"Is anyone else there with you? Besides Margot?"

"I see a woman with brown hair sitting on the grass."

"Is she your wife?"

"Yes . . . I don't know her," she added, referring to a recognition of someone in Catherine's present lifetime.

"Do you know Margot?" Look at Margot closely. Do you know her?"

"Yes, but I'm not sure how . . . I knew her from somewhere."

"It will come to you. Look into her eyes."

"It's Judy," she answered. Judy was presently Catherine's best friend. There had been an instant rapport at their first meeting, and they had become true friends, implicitly trusting each other, knowing the other's thoughts and needs before they were verbalized.

"Judy?" I repeated.

"Yes, Judy. She looks like her . . . she smiles like her."

"Yes, that's good. Are you happy at home, or are there problems?"

"There are no problems." [Long pause] "Yes. Yes, it is a time of unrest. There's a problem deep in the German government, the political structure. Too many people want to move in too many directions. It will eventually tear us apart. . . . But I must fight for my country."

"Do you have strong feelings for your country?"

"I dislike war. I feel it is wrong to kill, but I must do my duty."

"Go back now, back to where you were, to the plane on the ground, and the bombings, and the war. It's later; the war has started. The English and the Americans are dropping bombs near you. Go back. Do you see the plane again?"

"Yes."

"Do you still have the same feelings about duty and killing and war?"

"Yes, we will die for nothing."

"What?"

"We will die for nothing," she repeated in a louder whisper.

"Nothing? Why for nothing? Is there no glory in it? No defense of your land or your loved ones?"

"We will die for defending the ideas of a few people."

"Even though these were the leaders of your country? They can be wrong—" She quickly cut me off.

"They are not leaders. If they were leaders, there would not be so much internal strife . . . in government."

"Some people call them mad. Does this make sense to you? Power-crazy?"

"We must all be mad to be driven by them, to allow them to drive us . . . to kill people. And to kill ourselves. . . ."

"Have you any friends left?"

"Yes, there are still some alive."

"Are there any that you are particularly close to? In your airplane crew? Are your gunner and your navigator still alive?"

"I don't see them, but my plane wasn't destroyed."

"Do you fly again in the plane?"

"Yes, we must hurry to get the remaining aircraft off the strip . . . before they return."

"Go into your plane."

"I don't want to go." It was as if she could negotiate with me.

"But you must to get it off the ground."

"It's so senseless. . . ."

"What kind of profession did you have before the war? Do you remember? What did Eric do?"

"I was second in command . . . on a small plane, some plane flying cargo."

"So you were a pilot then, too?"

"Yes."

"That took you away from home a lot?"

She answered very softly, wistfully. "Yes."

"Go ahead in time," I instructed, "to the next flight. Can you do that?"

"There is no next flight."

"Does something happen to you?"

"Yes." Her breathing was accelerating, and she was becoming agitated. She had gone ahead to the day of her death.

"What's happening?"

"I'm running from the fire. My party's being torn apart by the fire."

"Do you survive this?"

"Nobody survives . . . nobody survives a war. I'm dying!" Her breathing was heavy. "Blood! Blood is everywhere! I have pain in my chest. I've been hit in my chest . . . and my leg . . . and my neck. It's so much pain. . . ." She was in agony; but soon her breathing slowed and became more regular; her facial muscles relaxed, and a look of peacefulness came over her. I recognized the calm of the transition state.

"You look more comfortable. Is it over?" She paused, then answered very softly.

"I'm floating . . . away from my body. I have no body. I am in spirit again."

"Good. Rest. You've had a difficult lifetime. You went through a difficult death. You need to rest. Restore yourself. What did you learn from that lifetime?"

"I learned about hate . . . senseless killing . . . misdirected hate . . . people who hate and they don't know why. We are driven to it . . . by the evil, when we are in physical state. . . ."

"Is there a higher duty than duty to the country? Something that could have prevented you from killing? Even if you were ordered? A duty to yourself?"

"Yes. . . ." But she did not elaborate.

"Are you waiting for something now?"

"Yes . . . I'm waiting to go into a state of renewal. I must wait. They will come for me . . . they will come. . . ."

"Good. I would like to talk with them when they come." We waited for several more minutes. Then abruptly her voice was loud and husky, and the original Master Spirit, not the poet Master, was speaking.

"You were correct in assuming this is the proper treatment for those in the physical state. You must eradicate the fears from their minds. It is a waste of energy when fear is present. It stifles them from fulfilling what they were sent here to fulfill. Take your cues from your surroundings. They must first be put into a level very, very deep . . . where they no longer can feel their body. Then you can reach them. It's only on the surface . . . that the troubles lie. Deep within their soul, where the ideas are created, that is where you must reach them.

"Energy . . . everything is energy. So much is wasted. The mountains . . . inside the mountain it is quiet; it is calm at the center. But on the outside is where the trouble lies. Humans can only see the outside, but you can go much deeper. You have to see the volcano. To do it you have to go deep inside.

"To be in physical state is abnormal. When you are in spiritual state, that is natural to you. When we are sent back, it's like being sent back to something we do not know. It will take us longer. In the spirit world you have to wait, and then you are renewed. There is a state of renewal. It's a dimension like the other dimensions, and you have almost succeeded in reaching that state. . . ."

This caught me by surprise. How could I be approaching the state of renewal? "I have almost reached it?" I asked incredulously.

"Yes. You know so much more than the others. You understand so much more. Be patient with them. They don't have the knowledge that you have. Spirits will be sent back to help you. But you are correct in what you are doing . . . continue. This energy must not be wasted. You must get rid of the fear. That will be the greatest weapon you have. . . ."

The Master Spirit was silent. I pondered the meaning of this incredible message. I knew I was successfully getting rid of Catherine's fears, but this message had a more global meaning. It was more than just a confirmation of the effectiveness of hypnosis as a therapeutic tool. It involved even more than past-life regressions, which would be difficult to apply to the general population, one by one. No, I believed it concerned the fear of death, which is the fear deep within the volcano. The fear of death, that hidden, constant fear that no amount of money or power can neutralize—this is the core. But if people knew that "life is endless; so we never die; we were never really born," then this fear would dissolve. If they knew that they had lived countless times before and would live countless times again, how reassured they would feel. If they knew that spirits were around to help them while they were in physical state and that after death, in spiritual state, they would join these spirits, including their deceased loved ones, how comforted they would be. If they knew that guardian "angels" really *did* exist, how much safer they would feel. If they knew that acts of violence and injustices against people did not go unnoted, but had to be repaid in kind in other lifetimes, how much less anger and desire for vengeance they would harbor. And if indeed, "by knowledge we approach God," of what use are material possessions, or power, when they are an end in themselves and not a means to that approach? To be greedy or power-hungry has no value whatsoever.

But how to reach people with this knowledge? Most people recite prayers in their churches, synagogues, mosques, or temples, prayers that proclaim the immortality of the soul. Yet after worship is over, they go back into their competitive ruts, practicing greed and manipulation and self-centeredness. These traits retard the progress of the soul. So, if faith is not enough, perhaps science will help. Perhaps experiences such as Catherine's and mine need to be studied, analyzed, and reported in a detached, scientific manner by people trained in the behavioral and physical sciences. Yet, at this time, writing a scientific paper or a book was the furthest thing from my mind, a remote and most unlikely possibility. I wondered about the spirits who would be sent back to help me. Help me do what?

Catherine stirred and began to whisper. "Someone named Gideon, someone named Gideon . . . Gideon. He's trying to talk to me."

"What does he say?"

"He's all around. He won't stop. He's some type of guardian . . . something. But he's playing with me now."

"Is he one of your guardians?"

"Yes, but he's playing . . . he's just jumping all around. I think he wants me to know he's all around me . . . everywhere."

"Gideon?" I repeated.

"He's there."

"Does it make you feel safer?"

"Yes. He'll be back when I need him."

"Good. Are there spirits around us?"

She answered in a whisper, from the perspective of her superconscious mind. "Oh, yes . . . many spirits. They only come when they want to. They come . . . when they want to. We are all spirits. But others . . . some are in physical state and others are in a period of renewal. And others are guardians. But we all go there. We have been guardians, too."

"Why do we come back to learn? Why can't we learn as spirits?"

"Those are different levels of learning, and we must learn some of them in the flesh. We must feel the pain. When you're a spirit you feel no pain. It is a period of renewal. Your soul is being renewed. When you're in physical state in the flesh, you can feel pain; you can hurt. In spiritual form you do not feel. There is only happiness, a sense of well-being. But it's a renewal period for . . . us. The interaction between people in the spiritual form is different. When you are in physical state . . . you can experience relationships."

"I understand. It will be okay." She had become silent again. Minutes passed.

"I see a carriage," she began, "a blue carriage."

"A baby carriage?"

"No, a carriage that you ride in. . . . Something blue! A blue fringe on the top, blue outside. . . ."

"Do horses pull the carriage?"

"It has big wheels. I don't see anybody in it, but just two horses hitched to it . . . a gray one and a brown one. The horse's name is Apple, the gray one, because he likes apples. The other one's name is Duke. They're very nice. They won't bite you. They have big feet . . . big feet."

"Is there a mean horse, too? A different horse?"

"No. They're very nice."

"Are you there?"

"Yes. I can see his nose. He's so much bigger than I am."

"Do you ride the carriage?" By the nature of her responses I knew she was a child.

"There are horses. There's a boy there, too."

"How old are you?"

"Very little. I don't know. I don't think I know how to count."

"Do you know the boy? Your friend? Your brother?"

"He's a neighbor. He's there for . . . some party. They're having a . . . wedding or something."

"Do you know who is getting married?"

"No. We were told not to get dirty. I have brown hair . . . shoes that button on the side all the way up."

"Are these your party clothes? Good clothes?"

"It's a white . . . some type of white dress with a . . . something ruffly over it, and it ties in the back."

"Is your house nearby?"

"It's a big house," the child answered.

"Is that where you live?"

"Yes."

"Good. You can look into the house now; it's okay. It's an important day. Other people will be dressed well, too, wearing special clothes."

"They're cooking food, lots of food."

"Can you smell it?"

"Yes. They're making some type of bread. Bread . . . meat. . . . We're told to go back outside again." I was amused at this. I had told her it was all right to go inside, and now she had been ordered out again.

"Do they call your name?"

". . . Mandy . . . Mandy and Edward."

"Is he the boy?"

"Yes."

"They won't let you stay in the house?"

"No, they're too busy."

"How do you feel about that?"

"We don't care. But it's hard to stay clean. We can't do anything."

"Do you get to the wedding? Later that day?"

"Yes . . . I see many people. It's crowded in the room. It's hot, a hot day. There's a parson there; the parson's there . . . with a funny hat, a big hat . . . black. It comes out over his face . . . quite a ways."

"Is this a happy time for your family?"

"Yes."

"Do you know who's getting married?"

"Just my sister."

"Is she much older?"

"Yes."

"Do you see her now? Is she wearing her wedding dress?"

"Yes."

"Is she pretty?"

"Yes. She has lots of flowers around her hair."

"Look at her closely. Do you know her from another time? Look at her eyes, her mouth. . . ."

"Yes. I think she's Becky . . . but smaller, much smaller." Becky was Catherine's friend and coworker. They were close, yet Catherine resented Becky's judgmental attitude and her intrusiveness into Catherine's life and decisions. After all, she was a friend, not family. But perhaps the distinction was now not so clear. "She . . . she likes me . . . and I can stand near the front because she does."

"Good. Look around you. Are your parents there?"

"Yes."

"Do they like you as much?"

"Yes."

"That's good. Look at them closely. First your mother. See if you remember her. Look at her face."

Catherine took several deep breaths. "I don't know her."

"Look at your father. Look at him closely. Look at his expression, his eyes . . . also his mouth. Do you know him?"

"He's Stuart," she quickly answered. So, Stuart had surfaced once again. This was worth exploring further.

"What's your relationship with him like?"

"I love him very much . . . he's very good to me. But he thinks I am a nuisance. He thinks children are nuisances."

"Is he too serious?"

"No, he likes to play with us. But we ask too many questions. But he's very good to us, except we ask too many questions."

"Does that sometimes annoy him?"

"Yes, we must learn from the teacher, not from him. That's why we go to school . . . to learn."

"That sounds like him talking. Does he say that to you?"

"Yes, he has more important things to do. He must run the farm."

"Is it a big farm?"

"Yes."

"Do you know where it is?"

"No."

"Do they ever mention the city or the state? The name of the town?"

She paused, listening carefully. "I don't hear that." She was silent again.

"Okay, do you want to explore more in this lifetime? To go ahead in time or is this—"

She cut me off. "This is enough."

During this entire process with Catherine, I had been reluctant to discuss her revelations with other professionals. Actually, except for Carole and a few others who were "safe," I had not shared this remarkable information with others at all. I knew the knowledge from our sessions was both true and extremely important, yet anxiety about the reactions of my professional and scientific colleagues caused me to keep silent. I was still concerned with my reputation, career, and what others thought of me.

My personal skepticism had been eroded by the proofs that, week after week, fell from her lips. I would often replay the audio tapes and reexperience the sessions, with all their drama and immediacy. But the others would have to rely on my experiences, powerful but nevertheless not their own. I felt compelled to gather even more data.

As I gradually accepted and believed the messages, my life became simpler and more satisfying. There was no need to play games, to pretend, to act out roles, or to be other than what I was. Relationships became more honest and direct. Family life was less confusing and more relaxed. My reluctance to share the wisdom that had been given to me through Catherine began to diminish. Surprisingly, most people were very interested and wanted to know more. Many told me of their very private experiences of parapsychological events, whether ESP, déjà vu, out-of-body experiences, past-life dreams, or others. Many had never even told their spouses about these experiences. People were almost uniformly afraid that, by sharing their experiences, others, even their own families and therapists, would consider them odd or strange. Yet these parapsychological events are fairly common, much more frequent than people realize. It is only the reluctance to tell others about psychic occurrences that makes them seem rare. And the more highly trained are the most reluctant to share.

The respected chairman of a major clinical department at my hospital is a man who is admired internationally for his expertise. He talks to his deceased father, who has several times protected him from serious danger. Another professor has dreams that provide the missing steps or solutions to his complex research experiments. The dreams are invariably correct. Another well-known doctor usually knows who is calling him on the phone before he answers it. The wife of the Chairman of Psychiatry at a midwestern university has a Ph.D. in psychology. Her research projects are always carefully planned and executed. She had never told anyone that when she first visited Rome, she moved through the city as if she had a road map imprinted in her memory. She unerringly knew what was around the next corner. Although she had never been to Italy previously and did not know the language, Italians repeatedly approached her in Italian, continually mistaking her for a native. Her mind struggled to integrate her experiences in Rome.

I understood why these highly trained professionals remained in the closet. I was one of them. We could not deny our own experiences and senses. Yet our training was in many ways diametrically opposite to the information, experiences, and beliefs we had accumulated. So we remained quiet.

Chapter
TEN

The week passed quickly. I had listened over and over again to the tape of last week's session. How was I approaching the state of renewal? I did not feel particularly enlightened. And now spirits would be sent back to help me. But what was I supposed to do? When would I find out? Would I be up to the task? I knew I must wait and be patient. I remembered the words of the poet Master.

"Patience and timing . . . everything comes when it must come. . . . Everything will be clear to you in time. But you must have a chance to digest the knowledge that we have given to you already." So I would wait.

At the beginning of this session Catherine related a fragment of a dream she had had several nights ago. In the dream she was living in her parents' house, and a fire had broken out during the night. She was in control, helping to evacuate the house, but her father was dawdling and seemingly indifferent to the urgency of the situation. She rushed him outside. Then he remembered something he had left in the house, and he sent Catherine back into the raging fire to retrieve the object. She could not remember what it was. I decided not to interpret the dream yet, but to wait and see if the opportunity would arise while she was hypnotized.

She quickly entered a deep hypnotic trance. "I see a woman

with a hood over her head, not covering her face, just on her hair." Then she was silent.

"Can you see that now? The hood?"

"I lost it. . . . I see some type of black material, brocade material with a gold design on it. . . . I see a building with some type of structural points on it . . . white."

"Do you recognize the building?"

"No."

"Is it a large building?"

"No. There's a mountain in the background with some snow on the top of it. But the grass is green in the valley . . . where we're at."

"Are you able to go into the building?"

"Yes. It's made of some type of marble . . . very cold to the touch."

"Is it some sort of temple or religious building?"

"I don't know. I thought it might be a prison."

"Prison?" I repeated. "Are there people in the building? Around it?"

"Yes, some soldiers. They have black uniforms, black with gold shoulder pads . . . gold tassels hanging off. Black helmets with some type of gold . . . something pointed and gold on the top . . . of the helmet. And a red sash, a red sash around the waist."

"Are there any soldiers around you?"

"Maybe two or three."

"Are you there?"

"I'm somewhere, but I'm not *in* the building. But I'm nearby."

"Look around. See if you can find yourself. . . . The mountains are there, and the grass . . . and the white building. Are there other buildings, too?"

"If there are other buildings, they're not situated near this one. I see one . . . isolated, with some type of wall built behind it . . . a wall."

"Do you think it's a fort or a prison or something like that?"

"It might be, but . . . it's very isolated."

"Why is that important to you?" [Long pause] "Do you know the name of the town or country where you are? Where the soldiers are?"

"I keep seeing 'Ukraine.' "

"Ukraine?" I repeated, fascinated by the diversity of her lifetimes. "Do you see a year? Does that come to you? Or a period of time?"

"Seventeen-seventeen," she answered hesitatingly, then corrected herself. "Seventeen fifty-eight . . . seventeen fifty-eight. There are many soldiers. I don't know what their purpose is. With long swords that curve."

"What else do you see or hear?" I inquired.

"I see a fountain, a fountain where they water the horses."

"Do the soldiers ride horses?"

"Yes."

"Are the soldiers known by any other name? Do they call themselves anything special?" She listened.

"I don't hear that."

"Are you among them?"

"No." Her answers were again a child's, short and often monosyllabic. I had to be a very active interviewer.

"But you're seeing them nearby?"

"Yes."

"Are you in the town?"

"Yes."

"Do you live there?"

"I believe so."

"Good. See if you can find yourself and where you live."

"I see some very ragged clothes. I see just a child, a boy. His clothes are ragged. He's cold. . . ."

"Does he have a home in the town?" There was a long pause.

"I don't see that," she continues. She seemed to be having some difficulty connecting with this lifetime. She was somewhat vague in her answers, somehow unsure.

"Okay. Do you know the boy's name?"

"No."

"What happens to the boy? Go with him. See what happens."

"Someone he knows is a prisoner."

"A friend? A relative?"

"I believe it's his father." Her answers were brief.

"Are you the boy?"

"I'm not sure."

"Do you know how he feels about his father being in prison?"

"Yes . . . he's very afraid, afraid they might kill him."

"What has his father done?"

"He has stolen something from the soldiers, some papers or something."

"The boy doesn't understand completely?"

"No. He might never see his father again."

"Can he get to see his father at all?"

"No."

"Do they know for how long his father will be in the prison? Or if he will live?"

"No!" she answered. Her voice quavered. She was very upset, very sad. She was not providing much detail, yet she was visibly agitated by the events she was witnessing and experiencing.

"You can feel what the boy is feeling," I went on, "that kind of fear and anxiety. Do you feel it?"

"Yes." Again, she was silent.

"What happens? Go ahead in time now. I know it's hard. Go ahead in time. Something happens."

"His father is executed."

"How does he feel now?"

"It was for something he never did. But they execute people for no reason at all."

"The boy must be very upset about this."

"I don't believe he understands fully . . . what has happened."

"Does he have other people to turn to?"

"Yes, but his life will be very hard."

"What becomes of the boy?"

"I don't know. He will probably die. . . ." She sounded so sad. She was again silent, then seemed to be looking around.

"What are you seeing?"

"I see a hand . . . a hand closing around something . . . white. I don't know what it is. . . ." She fell silent again, and minutes passed.

"What else do you see?" I asked.

"Nothing . . . darkness." She had either died or somehow disconnected from the sad boy who lived in the Ukraine more than two hundred years ago.

"Have you left the boy?"

"Yes," she whispered. She was resting.

"What did you learn from that lifetime? Why was it important?"

"People cannot be judged hastily. You have to be fair with someone. Many lives were ruined by being hasty in our judgments."

"The boy's life was short and hard because of that judgment . . . against his father."

"Yes." She was silent again.

"Are you seeing something else now? Do you hear anything?"

"No." Again there was the brief answer and then silence. For some reason, this brief lifetime had been particularly grueling. I gave her instructions to rest.

"Rest. Feel peacefulness. Your body is healing itself; your soul is resting. . . . Are you feeling better? Rested? It was difficult for the little boy. Very hard. But now you're resting again. Your mind can take you to other places, other times . . . other memories. Are you resting?"

"Yes." I decided to pursue the dream fragment about the burning house, her father's unconcerned dawdling, and his sending her back into the conflagration in order to retrieve something of his.

"I have a question now about the dream you had . . . with your father. You can remember it now; it's safe. You're in a deep trance. Do you remember?"

"Yes."

"You went back into the house to get something. Do you remember that?"

"Yes . . . it was a metal box."

"What was in it that he wanted so badly to send you back into a burning house?"

"His stamps and his coins . . . that he saves," she answered. Her detailed recollection of the dream content under hypnosis contrasted dramatically with her sketchy recall while awake. Hypnosis was a powerful tool, not only providing access to the most remote, hidden areas of the mind, but also allowing a much more detailed memory.

"Were his stamps and coins very important to him?"

"Yes."

"But to risk your life to go back into a burning house just for stamps and coins—"

She cut me off. "He didn't think he was risking it."

"He thought it was safe?"

"Yes."

"Then, why didn't he go back instead of you?"

"Because he thought I could go faster."

"I see. Was there a risk to you, though?"

"Yes, but he didn't realize that."

"Was there more meaning to that dream for you? About your relationship with your father?"

"I don't know."

"He didn't seem to be in much of a hurry to get out of the burning house."

"No."

"Why was he so leisurely? You were fast; you saw the danger."

"Because he tries to hide from things." I seized this moment to interpret part of the dream.

"Yes, it's an old pattern of his, and you do things for him, like fetching the box. I hope he can learn from you. I have a feeling that the fire represents time running out, that you realize the danger and that he doesn't. While he dawdles and sends you back for material objects, you know much more . . . and have much to teach him, but he doesn't seem to want to learn."

"No," she agreed. "He doesn't."

"That's how I see the dream. But you can't force him. Only he can realize this."

"Yes," she agreed again, and her voice became deep and husky, "it is unimportant that our bodies get burned in fires if we don't need them. . . ." A Master Spirit had shed an entirely different perspective on the dream. I was surprised at this sudden entrance, and I could only parrot back the thought.

"We don't need our bodies?"

"No. We go through so many stages when we're here. We shed a baby body, go into a child's, from child to an adult, an adult into old age. Why shouldn't we go one step beyond and shed the adult body and go on to a spiritual plane? That is what we do. We don't just stop growing; we continue to grow. When we get to the spiritual plane, we keep growing there, too. We go through different stages of development. When we arrive, we're burned out. We have to go through a renewal stage, a learning stage, and a stage of decision. We decide when we want to return, where, and for what reasons. Some choose not to come back. They choose to go on to another stage of development. And they stay in spirit form . . . some for longer than others before they return. It is all growth and learning . . . continuous growth. Our body is just a vehicle for us while we're here. It is our soul and our spirit that last forever."

I did not recognize the voice or style. A "new" Master was speaking, and speaking of important knowledge. I wanted to know more about these spiritual realms.

"Is learning in the physical state faster? Are there reasons that people don't all stay in the spiritual state?"

"No. Learning in the spiritual state is much faster, far accelerated from that in the physical state. But we choose what we need to learn. If we need to come back to work through a relationship, we come back. If we are finished with that, we go on. In spiritual form you can always contact those that are in physical state if you choose to. But only if there is importance there . . . if you have to tell them something that they must know."

"How do you make contact? How does the message come through?"

To my surprise, Catherine answered. Her whisper was faster and firmer. "Sometimes you can appear before that person . . . and look the same way you did when you were here. Other times you just make a mental contact. Sometimes the messages are cryptic, but most often the person knows what it pertains to. They understand. It's mind-to-mind contact."

I spoke to Catherine. "The knowledge that you have now, this information, this wisdom, which is very important . . . why is it not accessible to you when you are awake and in the physical state?"

"I guess I wouldn't understand it. I'm not capable of understanding it."

"Then, perhaps I can teach you to undertand it, so that it doesn't frighten you, and so that you learn."

"Yes."

"When you hear the voices of the Masters, they say things similar to what you are telling me now. You must share a great deal of information." I was intrigued at the wisdom she possessed when she was in this state.

"Yes," she replied simply.

"And this comes from your own mind?"

"But they have put it there." So she gave the credit to the Masters.

"Yes," I acknowledged. "How do I best communicate it back to you so that you grow and lose your fears?"

"You have already done that," she answered softly. She was right; her fears were nearly gone. Once the hypnotic regressions had begun, her clinical progress had been incredibly rapid.

"What lessons do you need to learn now? What is the most important thing you can learn during this lifetime so that you can continue to grow and prosper?"

"Trust," she answered quickly. She had known what her principal task was.

"Trust?" I repeated, surprised by the quickness of her retort.

"Yes. I must learn to have faith, but also to trust people. I don't. I think everybody is trying to do evil to me. That makes me stay away from people and situations that I probably shouldn't stay away from. It's keeping me with other people that I should break away from."

Her insight was tremendous when she was in this superconscious state. She knew her weaknesses and her strengths. She knew the areas that needed attention and work, and she knew what to do to improve matters. The only problem was that these insights needed to reach her conscious mind and needed to be applied to her waking life. Superconscious insight was fascinating, but by itself it was not enough to transform her life.

"Who are these people to break away from?" I asked.

She paused. "I am afraid of Becky. I'm afraid of Stuart . . . that somehow harm will come to me . . . from them."

"Can you break away from that?"

"Not completely, but from some of their ideas, yes. Stuart is trying to keep me in prison, and he is succeeding. He knows that I'm afraid. He knows I'm afraid to be away from him, and he uses that knowledge to keep me with him."

"And Becky?"

"She's constantly trying to break down my faith in the people that I have faith in. When I see good, she sees evil. And she tries to plant those seeds in my mind. I'm learning to trust . . . people I should trust, but she fills me with doubts about them. And that's her problem. I can't let her make me think her way."

In her superconscious state, Catherine was able to pinpoint major character flaws in both Becky and Stuart. The hypnotized Catherine would make an excellent psychiatrist, empathic and unerringly intuitive. The awake Catherine did not possess these attributes. It was my task to bridge the gulf. Her dramatic clinical improvement meant that some of this was seeping through. I attempted more bridge-building.

"Who can you trust?" I asked. "Think about it. Who are the people you can trust and learn from and get closer to. Who are they?"

"I can trust you," she whispered. I knew this, but I knew she needed to trust people in her everyday life even more.

"Yes, you can. You are close to me, but you must get closer to other people in your life, too, people who can be with you more than I can." I wanted her to be complete and independent, not dependent on me.

"I can trust my sister. I don't know the others. I can trust Stuart, but only to a certain extent. He does care about me, but he's confused. In his confusion he unknowingly is doing me harm."

"Yes, it is true. Is there another man that you can trust?"

"I can trust Robert," she answered. He was another physician in the hospital. They were good friends.

"Yes. Maybe there are still more for you to meet . . . in the future."

"Yes," she conceded.

The idea of future knowledge was distractingly intriguing. She had been so accurate about the past. She, through the Masters, had known specific, secret facts. Could they also know facts from the future? If so, could we share this foreknowledge? A thousand questions burst into my mind.

"When you find contact with your superconscious mind, like now, and have this wisdom, do you also develop abilities in the psychic realm? Is it possible for you to look into the future? We have done much in the past."

"That is possible," she conceded, "but I see nothing now."

"It is possible?" I echoed.

"I believe so."

"Can you do this without being frightened? Can you go into the future and obtain information of a neutral sort that will not be frightening to you? Can you see the future?"

Her answer was swift. "I don't see that. They will not allow it." I knew she meant the Masters.

"Are they around you now?"

"Yes."

"Are they talking to you?"

"No. They monitor everything." So, being monitored, she was not permitted to peer into the future. Perhaps we had nothing to gain personally from such a glimpse. Perhaps the adventure would have made Catherine too anxious. Perhaps we were not yet prepared to cope with this information. I did not push it.

"The spirit that was around you before, Gideon . . ."

"Yes."

"What does he need? Why is he near? Do you know him?"

"No, I don't believe so."

"But he protects you from danger?"

"Yes."

"The Masters. . . ."

"I don't see them."

"Sometimes they have messages for me, messages that help you and help me. Are these messages available to you even when they're not speaking? Do they put thoughts in your mind?"

"Yes."

"Do they monitor how far you can go? What you can remember?"

"Yes."

"So there is a purpose in this explanation of lifetimes. . . ."

"Yes."

". . . For you and for me . . . to teach us. To bring us the disappearance of fear."

"There are many ways of communication. They choose many . . . to show that they do exist." Whether Catherine was hearing their voices, visualizing past images and vistas, experiencing psychic phenomena, or having thoughts and ideas placed in her mind, the purpose was the same—to show that they do exist and, even beyond that, to help us, to aid us on our path by providing insights and knowledge, to help us become godlike through wisdom.

"Do you know why they have chosen you. . . ."

"No."

". . . to be a channel?"

This was a delicate question, since the awake Catherine could not even listen to the tapes. "No," she softly whispered.

"Does it frighten you?"

"Sometimes."

"And other times not?"

"Yes."

"It can be reassuring," I added. "We know now that we are eternal, so we lose our fear of death."

"Yes," she agreed. She paused. "I must learn to trust." She had returned to her lifetime's major lesson. "When I'm told something, I must learn to trust what I am told . . . when the person is knowledgeable."

"Certainly there are people not to trust," I added.

"Yes, but I'm confused. And the people I know I should

trust, I fight against that feeling. And I don't want to trust anybody." She was silent as I again admired her insight.

"Last time we talked about you as a child, in a garden with horses. Do you remember? Your sister's wedding?"

"A little."

"Was there more to gather from that time? Do you know?"

"Yes."

"Would it be worthwhile to go back now and explore it?"

"It won't come back now. There are so many things in a lifetime . . . there is so much knowledge to attain . . . from each lifetime. Yes, we must explore, but it won't come back now."

So I turned again to her troubled relationship with her father. "Your relationship with your father is another area, one that has affected you deeply in this life."

"Yes," she answered simply.

"It is another area to explore yet, too. You've had much to learn from this relationship. Compare it to the little boy in the Ukraine who lost his father at an early age. And this loss did not happen to you this time. And yet, having your father here, even though certain hardships were less . . ."

"Was more of a burden," she concluded. "Thoughts . . ." she added, "thoughts. . . ."

"What thoughts?" I sensed she was in a new area.

"About the anesthesia. When they give you anesthesia, can you hear? You *can* still hear!" She had answered her own question. She was whispering rapidly now, becoming excited. "Your mind is very much aware of what's going on. They were talking about my choking, about the possibility of me choking when they did the surgery on my throat."

I remembered Catherine's vocal cord surgery, which was performed just a few months before her first appointment with me. She had been anxious prior to the surgery, but she was absolutely terrified upon awakening in the recovery room. It had taken the nursing staff hours to calm her. Now it appeared that what was said by the surgeons during the operation, during the time she was under deep anesthesia, had precipitated her terror. My mind flipped back to medical school and my surgery rotation. I remembered the casual conversations during operations, while the patients were anesthetized. I remembered the jokes, the cursing, the arguments, and the surgeons' temper tantrums. What had the patients heard, at a subconscious level? How much registered to affect their thoughts and emotions, their fears and anxieties, after they awakened? Was the postoperative course, the patient's very recovery from the surgery, influenced positively or negatively by the remarks made during the operation? Had anyone died because of negative expectations overheard during surgery? Had they, feeling hopeless, just given up?

"Do you remember what they were saying?" I asked.

"That they had to put a tube down. When they took the tube out, my throat might swell up. They didn't think I could hear."

"But you did."

"Yes. That's why I had all the problems." After today's session, Catherine no longer had any fear of swallowing or choking. It was as simple as that. "All the anixety . . ." she continued, "I thought I would choke."

"Do you feel free?" I asked.

"Yes. You can reverse what they did."

"Can I?"

"Yes. You *are*. . . . They should be very careful of what they say. I remember it now. They put a tube in my throat. And then I couldn't talk afterward to tell them anything."

"Now you're free. . . . You did hear them."

"Yes, I heard them talk. . . ." She fell silent for a minute or two, then began to turn her head from side to side. She seemed to be listening to something.

"You seem to be hearing messages. Do you know where that message came from? I was hoping the Masters would appear."

"Someone told me" was her cryptic answer.

"Somebody was speaking to you?"

"But they're gone." I tried to bring them back.

"See if you can bring back spirits with messages for us . . . to help us out."

"They come only when they want to, not when I choose," she answered firmly.

"You don't have any control over it?"

"No."

"Okay," I conceded, "but the message about the anesthesia was very important for you. That was the source of your choking."

"It was important for you, not me," she retorted. Her answer reverberated through my mind. *She* would be cured of the terror of choking, yet this revelation was nevertheless more important for me than for her. I was the one doing the healing. Her simple answer contained many levels of meaning. I felt that if I truly understood these levels, these resonating octaves of meanings, I would advance a quantum leap into the understanding of human relationships. Perhaps the helping was more important than the cure.

"For me to help you?" I asked.

"Yes. You can undo what they did. You *have* been undoing what they did. . . ." She was resting. We had both learned a great lesson.

• • •

Shortly after her third birthday my daughter, Amy, came running over to me, hugging me around the legs. She looked up and said, "Daddy, I've loved you for forty thousand years." I looked down at her little face, and I felt very, very happy.

Chapter
ELEVEN

Several nights later I was jolted awake from a deep sleep. Instantly alert, I had a vision of Catherine's face, several times larger than life-size. She looked upset, as if she needed my help. I looked over at the clock; it was 3:36 A.M. There had been no outside noises to awaken me. Carole was sleeping peacefully beside me. I dismissed the incident and fell back to sleep.

At about 3:30 that same morning, Catherine had awakened in a panic from a nightmare. She was sweating and her heart was racing. She decided to meditate to relax, visualizing my hypnotizing her in the office. She pictured my face, heard my voice, and gradually fell back to sleep.

Catherine was becoming increasingly psychic, and apparently so was I. I could hear my old psychiatry professors talking about transference and countertransference reactions in therapeutic relationships. Transference is the patient's projection of feelings, thoughts, and wishes onto the therapist, who represents someone from the patient's past. Countertransference is the reverse, the therapist's unconscious emotional reactions to the patient. But this 3:30 A.M. communication was neither. This was a telepathic bond along a wavelength outside the normal channels. Somehow the hypnosis was opening up this channel. Or was it the audience, a diverse group of spirits—Masters and guardians and others—that was responsible for the new wavelength? I was beyond the point of surprise.

In the next session, Catherine quickly reached a deep hypnotic level. She was instantly alarmed. "I see a big cloud . . . it scared me. It was there." She was breathing rapidly.

"Is it still there?"

"I don't know. It came and went quickly . . . something up high on a mountain." She remained alarmed, continuing to breathe heavily. I was afraid she was seeing a bomb. Could she look into the future?

"Can you see the mountain? Is it like a bomb?"

"I don't know."

"Why did it scare you?"

"It was very sudden. It was just there. It's very smoky . . . very smoky. It's big. It's off at a distance. Oh. . . ."

"You're safe. Can you get closer to it?"

"I don't want to get closer!" she answered sharply. It was rare for her to be so resistant.

"Why are you so afraid of it?" I asked again.

"I think it's some chemicals or something. It's hard to breathe when you're around it." She was breathing laboriously.

"Is it like a gas? Is it coming from the mountain itself . . . like a volcano?"

"I think so. It's like a big mushroom. That's what it looks like . . . a white one."

"But not a bomb? It's not an atomic bomb or anything like that?" She paused and then continued.

"It's a vol . . . some type of volcano or something, I think. It's very scary. It's hard to breathe. There's dust in the air. I don't want to be there." Slowly her breathing returned to the usual deep and even respirations of the hypnotic state. She had left this frightening scene.

"Is it easier to breathe now?"

"Yes."

"Good. What are you seeing now?"

"Nothing. . . . I see a necklace, a necklace on somebody's neck. It's blue . . . it's silver and has a blue stone hanging off it, and then littler stones underneath that."

"Is there anything on the blue stone?"

"No, it's see-through. You can see through it. The lady has black hair and a blue hat on . . . with a big feather, and the dress is velvet."

"Do you know the lady?"

"No."

"Are you there, or are you the lady?"

"I don't know."

"But you see her?"

"Yes. I'm not the lady."

"How old is she?"

"In her forties. But she looks older than what she is."

"Is she doing anything?"

"No, she's just standing next to the table. There's a perfume bottle on the table. It's white with green flowers on it. There's a brush and a comb with silver handles." I was impressed with her eye for detail.

"Is it her room, or is it in a store?"

"It's her room. There's a bed in it . . . with four posts on it. It's a brown bed. There's a pitcher on the table."

"A pitcher?"

"Yes, there are no pictures in the room. There are funny, dark curtains."

"Is anybody else around?"

"No."

"What relationship does this lady have to you?"

"I serve her." Once again she was a servant.

"Have you been with her long?"

"No . . . a few months."

"Do you like that necklace?"

"Yes. She's very elegant."

"Have you ever worn the necklace?"

"No." Her short answers required my active steering in order to obtain basic information. She reminded me of my preteenage son.

"How old are you now?"

"Maybe thirteen, fourteen. . . ." About the same age.

"Why have you left your family?" I inquired.

"I haven't left them," she corrected me. "I just work there."

"I see. Do you go home to your family after that?"

"Yes." Her answers left little room for exploration.

"Do they live nearby?"

"Close enough. . . . We are very poor. It is necessary for us to work . . . to serve."

"Do you know the lady's name?"

"Belinda."

"Does she treat you well?"

"Yes."

"Good. Do you work hard?"

"It's not very tiring." Interviewing teenagers was never easy, even in past lifetimes. It was fortunate that I was well practiced.

"Good. Are you still seeing her now?"

"No."

"Where are you now?"

"In another room. There's a table with a black covering on it . . . and fringe around the bottom. It smells of many herbs . . . heavy perfume."

"Does this all belong to your mistress? Does she use a lot of perfume?"

"No, this is another room. I'm in another room."

"Whose room is this?"

"It belongs to some dark lady."

"Dark how? Can you see her?"

"She has many coverings on her head," Catherine whispered, "many shawls. She's old and wrinkled."

"What is your relationship to her?"

"I've just gone to see her."

"For what?"

"So she may do the cards." Intuitively I knew that she had gone to a fortune teller, one who probably read tarot cards. This was an ironic twist. Here Catherine and I were involved in an incredible psychic adventure, spanning lifetimes and dimensions beyond even that, and yet, perhaps two hundred years earlier, she had visited a psychic to find out about her future. I knew that Catherine had never visited a psychic in her present life, and she had no knowledge whatsoever about tarot cards or fortune-telling; these things frightened her.

"Does she read fortunes?" I asked.

"She sees things."

"Do you have a question for her? What do you want to see? What do you want to know?"

"About some man . . . that I might marry."

"What does she say when she does the cards?"

"The card with . . . some kind of poles on it. Poles and flowers . . . but poles, spears, or some kind of line. There's another card with a chalice on it, a cup. . . . I see a card with a man or boy carrying a shield. She says I will marry, but I will not marry this man. . . . I see nothing else."

"Do you see the lady?"

"I see some coins."

"Are you still with her, or is this a different place?"

"I am with her."

"What do the coins look like?"

"They're gold. The edges are not smooth. They are squared. There's a crown on one side."

"See if there is a year imprinted on the coins. Something that you can read . . . in lettering."

"Some foreign numbers," she replied. "X's and I's."

"Do you know what year that is?"

"Seventeen . . . something. I don't know when." She was silent again.

"Why is this fortune-teller important to you?"

"I don't know. . . ."

"Does her fortune come true?"

". . . But she's gone," Catherine whispered. "It's gone. I don't know."

"Do you see anything now?"

"No."

"No?" I was surprised. Where was she? "Do you know your name in this lifetime?" I asked, hoping to pick up the thread of this life several hundred years ago.

"I'm gone from there." She had left the lifetime and was resting. She could do this now on her own. It was not necessary for her to experience her death to do so. We waited for several minutes. This lifetime had not been spectacular. She had remembered only some descriptive highlights and the interesting visit to the fortune-teller.

"Do you see anything now?" I asked again.

"No," she whispered.

"Are you resting?"

"Yes . . . jewels of different colors. . . ."

"Jewels?"

"Yes. They're really lights, but they look like jewels. . . ."

"What else?" I asked.

"I just . . ." she paused, and then her whisper was loud and firm. "There are many words and thoughts that are flying around. . . . It's about coexistence and harmony . . . the balance of things." I knew the Masters were nearby.

"Yes," I urged her on. "I want to know about these things. Can you tell me?"

"Right now they're just words," she answered.

"Coexistence and harmony," I reminded her. When she answered, it was the voice of the poet Master. I was thrilled to hear from him again.

"Yes," he answered. "Everything must be balanced. Nature is balanced. The beasts live in harmony. Humans have not learned to do that. They continue to destroy themselves. There is no harmony, no plan to what they do. It's so different in nature. Nature is balanced. Nature is energy and life . . . and restoration. And humans just destroy. They destroy nature. They destroy other humans. They will eventually destroy themselves."

This was an ominous prediction. With the world constantly in chaos and turmoil, I hoped this would not be soon. "When will this happen?" I asked.

"It will happen sooner than they think. Nature will survive. Plants will survive. But we will not."

"Can we do anything to prevent that destruction?"

"No. Everything must be balanced. . . ."

"Will this destruction happen in our lifetime? Can we avert it?"

"It will not happen in our lifetime. We will be on another plane, another dimension, when it happens, but we will see it."

"Is there no way of teaching humankind?" I kept looking for a way out, for some mitigating possibility.

"It will be done on another level. We will learn from that."

I looked on the bright side. "Well, then our souls progress in different places."

"Yes. We will no longer be . . . here, as we know it. We will see it."

"Yes," I conceded. "I have a need to teach these people, but I don't know how to reach them. Is there a way, or do they have to learn this for themselves?"

"You cannot reach everyone. In order to stop the destruction you must reach everyone, and you cannot. It cannot be stopped. They will learn. When they progress, they will learn. There will be peace, but not here, not here in this dimension."

"Eventually there will be peace?"

"Yes, on another level."

"It seems so far away, though," I complained. "People seem so petty now . . . greedy, power-hungry, ambitious. They forget about love and understanding and knowledge. There is much to learn."

"Yes."

"Can I write anything to help these people? Is there some way?"

"You know the way. We do not have to tell you. It will all be to no avail, for we will all reach the level, and they will see. We are all the same. One is no greater than the next. And all this is just lessons . . . and punishments."

"Yes," I agreed. This lesson was a profound one, and I needed time to digest it. Catherine had become silent. We waited, she resting and I pensively absorbed in the dramatic pronouncements of the past hour. Finally, she broke the spell.

"The jewels are gone," she whispered. "The jewels are gone. The lights . . . they're gone."

"The voices, too? The words?"

"Yes. I see nothing." As she paused, her head began to move from side to side. "A spirit . . . is looking."

"At you?"

"Yes."

"Do you recognize the spirit?"

"I'm not sure . . . I think it might be Edward." Edward had died during the previous year. Edward was truly ubiquitous. He seemed to be always around her.

"What did the spirit look like?"

"Just a . . . just white . . . like lights. He had no face, not like we know it, but I know it's he."

"Was he communicating at all with you?"

"No, he was just watching."

"Was he listening to what I was saying?"

"Yes," she whispered. "But he's gone now. He just wanted to be sure I'm all right." I thought about the popular mythology of the guardian angel. Certainly Edward, in the role of the hovering, loving spirit watching over her to make sure she was all right, approached such an angelic role. And Catherine had already talked about guardian spirits. I wondered how many of our childhood "myths" were actually rooted in a dimly remembered past.

I also wondered about the hierarchy of spirits, about who became a guardian and who a Master, and about those who were neither, just learning. There must be gradations based upon wisdom and knowledge, with the ultimate goal that of becoming God-like and approaching, perhaps merging somehow, with God. This was the goal that mystic theologians had described in ecstatic terms over the centuries. They had had glimpses of such a divine union. Short of such personal experience, vehicles such as Catherine, with her extraordinary talent, provided the best view.

Edward had gone, and Catherine had become silent. Her

face was peaceful, and she was enveloped in serenity. What a
marvelous talent she possessed—the ability to see beyond life
and beyond death, to talk with the "gods" and to share their
wisdom. We were eating from the Tree of Knowledge, no
longer forbidden. I wondered how many apples were left.

Carole's mother, Minette, was dying from the cancer that
had spread from her breast to her bones and liver. The process
had been going on for four years and now could no longer be
slowed down by chemotherapy. She was a brave woman who
stoically endured the pain and weakness. But the disease was
accelerating, and I knew that her death was approaching.

The sessions with Catherine were going on simultaneously,
and I shared the experience and revelations with Minette. I
was mildly surprised that she, a practical businesswoman,
readily accepted this knowledge and wanted to learn more. I
gave her books to read, and she did so avidly. She arranged
for and took a course with Carole and me in kabbalah,
the Jewish mystical writings that are centuries old. Reincarnation and the in-between planes are basic tenets of kabbalistic
literature, yet most modern-day Jews are unaware of this.
Minette's spirit strengthened as her body deteriorated. Her
fear of death diminished. She began to anticipate being reunited with her beloved husband, Ben. She believed in the
immortality of her soul, and this helped her endure the pain.
She was holding on to life, awaiting the birth of another
grandchild, her daughter Donna's first baby. She had met
Catherine in the hospital during one of her treatments, and
their eyes and words joined peacefully and eagerly. Catherine's
sincerity and honesty helped convince Minette that the existence of an afterlife was indeed true.

A week before she died, Minette was admitted to the hospital's oncology floor. Carole and I were able to spend time with her, talking about life and death, and what awaited us all after death. A lady of great dignity, she decided to die in the hospital, where the nurses could care for her. Donna, her husband, and their six-week-old daughter came to spend time with her and say good-bye. We were almost continuously with her. About six in the evening of the night Minette died, Carole and I, having just arrived home from the hospital, both experienced a strong urge to go back. The next six or seven hours were filled with serenity and a transcendental spiritual energy. Although her breathing was labored, Minette had no more pain. We talked about her transition to the in-between state, the bright light, and the spiritual presence. She reviewed her life, mostly silently, and struggled to accept the negative parts. She seemed to know that she couldn't let go until this process was completed. She was waiting for a very specific time to die, in the early morning. She grew impatient for this time to come. Minette was the first person I had guided to and through death in this manner. She was strengthened, and our grief was assuaged by the entire experience.

I found that my ability to heal my patients had significantly expanded, not just with phobias and anxieties, but especially in death-and-dying, or grief, counseling. I intuitively knew what was wrong and what directions to take in therapy. I was able to convey feelings of peacefulness, calm, and hope. After Minette's death, many others who were either dying or who were the survivors of a loved one's death came for help. Many were not ready to know about Catherine or the literature about life after death. But even without imparting such specific knowledge, I felt that I could still deliver the message. A tone of voice, an empathic understanding of the process and of their fears and feelings, a look, a touch, a word— all could get through, at some level, and touch a chord of hope, of forgotten spirituality, of shared humanity, or even more. And for those ready for more, to suggest readings and to share my experiences with Catherine and others was like opening a window to a fresh breeze. The ones who were ready were revived. They gained insights even more rapidly.

I believe strongly that therapists must have open minds. Just as more scientific work is necessary to document death-and-dying experiences, such as Catherine's, so is more experiential work necessary in the field. Therapists need to consider the possibility of life after death and integrate it into their counseling. They do not have to use hypnotic regressions, but they should keep their minds open, share their knowledge with their patients, and not discount their patients' experiences.

People are now devastated by threats to their mortality. The plague of AIDS, nuclear holocaust, terrorism, disease, and many other catastrophes hang over our heads and torture us daily. Many teenagers believe that they won't live past their twenties. This is incredible, reflecting the tremendous stresses in our society.

On the individual level, Minette's reaction to Catherine's messages is encouraging. Her spirit had strengthened, and she had felt hope in the face of great physical pain and bodily deterioration. But the messages are for all of us, not just the dying. There is hope for us, too. We need more clinicians and scientists to report on other Catherines, to confirm and expand her messages. The answers are there. We are immortal. We will always be together.

Chapter
TWELVE

Three and a half months had passed since our first hypnosis session. Not only had Catherine's symptoms virtually disappeared, but she had progressed beyond merely being cured. She was radiant, with a peaceful energy around her. People were drawn to her. When she ate breakfast in the hospital cafeteria, both men and women would rush to join her. "You look so beautiful; I just wanted to tell you that," they would say. Like a fisher, she would reel them in on an invisible psychic line. And she had been eating unnoticed in the same cafeteria for years.

As usual, she sank quickly into a deep hypnotic trance in my dimly lit office, her blond hair spilling over in rivulets on the familiar beige pillow.

"I see a building . . . it's made out of stone. And there's something pointed on the top of it. It's in a very mountainous area. It's very damp . . . it's very damp outside. I see a wagon. I see a wagon going by . . . the front. The wagon has hay in it, some kind of straw or hay or something for the animals to eat. There are some men there. They're carrying some type of banners, something flying on the end of a stick. Very bright colors. I hear them talking about Moors . . . Moors. And a war that's being fought. There's some type of metal, something metal covering their heads . . . some type of head covering made of metal. The year is 1483. Something about Danes. Are we fighting the Danes? Some war is being fought."

"Are you there?" I questioned.

"I don't see that," she answered softly. "I see the wagons. They have two wheels on them, two wheels and an open back. They're open; the sides are open with slats, some type of wooden slats held together. I see . . . something metal they wear around their necks . . . very heavy metal in the shape of a cross. But the ends are curved, the ends are round . . . on the cross. It's the feast of some saint. . . . I see swords. They have some type of knife or sword . . . very heavy, very blunt end. They are preparing for some battle."

"See if you can find yourself," I instructed. "Look around. Perhaps you're a soldier. You're seeing them from somewhere."

"I'm not a soldier." She was definite about this.

"Look around."

"I have brought some of the provisions. It's a village, some village." She was silent.

"What do you see now?"

"I see a banner, some type of banner. It's red and white . . . white with a red cross."

"Is it the banner of your people?" I asked.

"It's the banner of the king's soldiers," she responded.

"Is this your king?"

"Yes."

"Do you know the king's name?"

"I don't hear that. He's not there."

"Can you look and see what you're wearing? Look down and see what you're wearing."

"Some type of leather . . . leather tunic over . . . over

a very rough shirt. A leather tunic . . . it's short. Some type of animal-skin shoes . . . not shoes, more like boots or moccasins. No one's talking to me."

"I understand. What color is your hair?"

"It's light, but I'm old, and there's some gray to it."

"How do you feel about this war?"

"It has become my way of life. I've lost a child in a previous skirmish."

"A son?"

"Yes." She was sad.

"Who's left for you? Who's left in your family?"

"My wife . . . and my daughter."

"What was your son's name?"

"I don't see his name. I remember him. I see my wife." Catherine had been both male and female many times. Childless in her present life, she had parented numerous children in her other lifetimes.

"What does your wife look like?"

"She's very tired, very tired. She's old. We have some goats."

"Does your daughter still live with you?"

"No, she is married and left some time ago."

"Are you alone, then, you and your wife?"

"Yes."

"How is your life?"

"We are tired. We are very poor. It has not been easy."

"No. You've lost your son. Do you miss him?"

"Yes," she answered simply, but the grief was palpable.

"Have you been a farmer?" I changed the subject.

"Yes. There's wheat . . . wheat, something like wheat."

"Have there been many wars in your land, through your life, with much tragedy?"

"Yes."

"But you have lived to be old."

"But they fight away from the village, not *in* the village," she explained. "They must travel to where they do battle . . . over many mountains."

"Do you know the name of the land that you live in? Or the town?"

"I don't see it, but it must have a name. I don't see it."

"Is this a very religious time for you? You see crosses on the soldiers."

"For others, yes. Not for me."

"Is anybody alive yet from the rest of your family, other than your wife and your daughter?"

"No."

"Your parents have died?"

"Yes."

"Brothers and sisters?"

"I have a sister. She is alive. I don't know her," she added, referring to her life as Catherine.

"Okay. See if you recognize anyone else in the village or your family." If people did reincarnate in groups, she was likely to find someone there who was also significant in her current lifetime.

"I see a stone table . . . I see bowls."

"Is this your house?"

"Yes. Something made out of ker . . . something yellow, something from corn . . . or something . . . yellow. We eat this. . . ."

"All right," I added, trying to quicken the pace. "This has been a very hard life for you, a very hard life. What are you thinking of?"

"Horses," she whispered.

"Do you own horses? Or does somebody else?"

"No, soldiers . . . some of them. Mostly they walk. But they're not horses; they're donkeys or something littler than horses. They are mostly wild."

"Go ahead in time now," I instructed. "You're very old. Try to go to the last day in your lifetime as an old man."

"But I'm not very old," she objected. She was not particularly suggestible in these past lives. What was happening was happening. I could not suggest away the actual memories. I could not get her to change the details of what had happened and been remembered.

"Is there more to happen in this lifetime?" I asked, changing my approach. "It is important for us to know."

"Nothing of significance," she answered without emotion.

"Then, go ahead, go ahead in time. Let's find out what you needed to learn. Do you know?"

"No. I'm still there."

"Yes, I know. Are you seeing something?" A minute or two passed before she answered.

"I'm just floating," she whispered softly.

"Have you left him now?"

"Yes, I'm floating." She had entered the spiritual state again.

"Do you know now what you needed to learn? It was another hard lifetime for you."

"I don't know. I'm just floating."

"Okay. Rest . . . rest." More minutes passed silently. Then she seemed to be listening to something. Abruptly she spoke. Her voice was loud and deep. This was not Catherine.

"There are seven planes in all, seven planes, each one consisting of many levels, one of them being the plane of recollection. On that plane you are allowed to collect your thoughts. You are allowed to see your life that has just passed. Those of the higher levels are allowed to see history. They can go back and teach us by learning about history. But we of the lower levels are only allowed to see our own life . . . that has just passed.

"We have debts that must be paid. If we have not paid out these debts, then we must take them into another life . . . in order that they may be worked through. You progress by paying your debts. Some souls progress faster than others. When you're in physical form and you are working through, you're working through a life. . . . If something interrupts your ability . . . to pay that debt, you must return to the plane of recollection, and there you must wait until the soul you owe the debt to has come to see you. And when you both can be returned to physical form at the same time, then you are allowed to return. But you determine when you are going back. You determine what must be done to pay that debt. You will not remember your other lives . . . only the one you have just come from. Only those souls on the higher level—the sages—are allowed to call upon history and past events . . . to help us, to teach us what we must do.

"There are seven planes . . . seven through which we must pass before we are returned. One of them is the plane of transition. There you wait. In that plane it is determined what you will take back with you into the next life. We will all have . . . a dominant trait. This might be greed, or it might be lust, but whatever is determined, you need to fulfill your debts to those people. Then you must overcome this in that lifetime. You must learn to overcome greed. If you do not, when you return you will have to carry that trait, as well as another one, into your next life. The burdens will become greater. With each life that you go through and you did not fulfill these debts, the next one will be harder. If you fulfill them, you will be given an easy life. So you choose what life you will have. In the next phase, you are responsible for the life you have, You choose it." Catherine fell silent.

This was apparently not from a Master. He identified himself as "we of the lower levels," in comparison with those souls on the higher level—"the sages." But the knowledge transmitted was both clear and practical. I wondered about the five other planes and their qualities. Was the stage of renewal one of those planes? And what about the learning stage and the stage of decisions? All of the wisdom revealed through these messages from souls in various dimensions of the spiritual state was consistent. The style of delivery differed, the phraseology and grammar differed, the sophistication of verse and vocabulary differed; but the content remained coherent. I was acquiring a systematic body of spiritual knowledge. This knowledge spoke of love and hope, faith and charity. It examined virtues and vices, debts owed to others and to one's self. It included past lifetimes and spiritual planes between lives. And it talked of the soul's progress through harmony and balance, love and wisdom, progress toward a mystical and ecstatic connection with God.

There was much practical advice along the way: the value of patience and of waiting; the wisdom in the balance of nature; the eradication of fears, especially the fear of death; the need for learning about trust and forgiveness; the importance of learning not to judge others, or to halt anyone's life; the accumulation and use of intuitive powers; and, perhaps most of all, the unshakable knowledge that we are immortal. We are beyond life and death, beyond space and beyond time. We are the gods, and they are us.

"I'm floating," Catherine was whispering softly.

"What state are you in?" I asked.

"Nothing . . . I'm floating. . . . Edward owes me something . . . he owes me something."

"Do you know what he owes you?"

"No. . . . Some knowledge . . . he owes me. He had something to tell me, maybe about my sister's child."

"Your sister's child?" I echoed.

"Yes . . . it's a girl. Her name is Stephanie."

"Stephanie? What do you need to know about her?"

"I need to know how to get in touch with her," she answered. Catherine had never mentioned anything to me about this niece.

"Is she very close to you?" I asked.

"No, but she'll want to find them."

"Find who?" I questioned. I was confused.

"My sister and her husband. And the only way she can do that is through me. I'm the link. He has information. Her father is a doctor; he's practicing somewhere in Vermont, the southern part of Vermont. The information will come to me when it's needed."

I later learned that Catherine's sister and her sister's future husband had put their infant daughter up for adoption. They were teenagers at that time, and they were not yet married. The adoption was arranged by the Church. There was no information available after that time.

"Yes," I agreed. "When it's the right time."

"Yes. Then he will tell me. He'll tell me."

"What other information does he have for you?"

"I don't know, but he has things to tell me. And he owes me something . . . something. I don't know what. He owes me something." She was silent.

"Are you tired?" I asked.

"I see a bridle" was her whispered reply. "Tackle on the wall. A bridle . . . I see a blanket lying on the outside of a stall."

"Is it a barn?"

"They have horses there. They have many horses."

"What else do you see?"

"I see many trees—with yellow flowers. My father is there. He takes care of the horses." I realized I was talking to a child.

"What does he look like?"

"He's very tall, with gray hair."

"Do you see yourself?"

"I'm a child . . . a girl."

"Does your father own the horses or just take care of them?"

"He just takes care of them. We live nearby."

"Do you like horses?"

"Yes."

"Do you have a favorite?"

"Yes. My horse. His name is Apple." I remembered her lifetime as Mandy, when a horse named Apple had also appeared. Was she again repeating a lifetime we had already experienced? Perhaps she was approaching it from another perspective.

"Apple . . . yes. Does your father let you ride Apple?"

"No, but I can feed him things. He's used for pulling the master's wagon, pulling his carriage. He's very big. He has big feet. If you're not careful, he'll step on you."

"Who else is with you?"

"My mother is there. I see a sister . . . she's bigger than me. I don't see anyone else."

"What do you see now?"

"I just see the horses."

"Is this a happy time for you?"

"Yes. I like the smell of the barn." She was being very specific, referring to that moment in time, in the barn.

"Do you smell the horses?"

"Yes."

"The hay?"

"Yes . . . their faces are so soft. There are dogs there, too . . . black ones, some black ones and some cats . . . lots of animals. The dogs are used for hunting. When they hunt for birds, the dogs are allowed to go."

"Does anything happen to you?"

"No." My question was too vague.

"Do you grow up on this farm?"

"Yes. The man who is taking care of the horses." She paused. "He's not really my father." I was confused.

"He's not your real father?"

"I don't know, he's . . . he's not my real father, no. But he is like a father to me. He's a second father. He is very good to me. He has green eyes."

"Look in his eyes—green eyes—and see if you can recognize him. He's good to you. He loves you."

"He's my grandfather . . . my grandfather. He loved us very much. My grandfather loved us very much. He used to take us out with him all the time. We used to go with him to where he would drink. And we could get sodas. He liked us." My question had jolted her out of that lifetime into her observing, superconscious state. She was viewing Catherine's life now and her relationship with her grandfather.

"Do you still miss him?" I asked.

"Yes," she answered softly.

"But you see he has been with you before." I was explaining, trying to minimize her hurt.

"He was very good to us. He loved us. He never hollered at us. He used to give us money and take us with him all the time. He liked that. But he died."

"Yes, but you'll be with him again. You know that."

"Yes. I've been with him before. He was not like my father. They're so different."

"Why does one love you so much and treat you so well, and the other one is so different?"

"Because one has learned. He has paid a debt he has owed. My father has not paid his debt. He has come back . . . without understanding. He will have to do it again."

"Yes," I agreed. "He has to learn to love, to nurture."

"Yes," she answered.

"If they don't understand this," I added, "they treat children like property, instead of like people to love."

"Yes," she agreed.

"Your father still has to learn this."

"Yes."

"Your grandfather already knows. . . ."

"I know," she interjected. We have so many stages we go through when we're in physical state . . . just like the other stages of evolution. We have to go through the infancy stage, the baby stage, the child stage. . . . We have so far to go before we reach . . . before we reach our goal. The stages in physical form are hard. Those in the astral plane are easy. There we just rest and wait. These are the hard stages now."

"How many planes are there in the astral state?"

"There are seven," she answered.

"What are they," I questioned, looking to confirm those beyond the two mentioned earlier in the session.

"I've only been told two," she explained. "The transition stage and the stage of recollection."

"Those are the two that I'm familiar with, also."

"We will know the others later."

"You have learned at the same time I did," I observed. "We learned today about debts. It is very important."

"I will remember what I should remember," she added enigmatically.

"Will you remember these planes?" I inquired.

"No. They aren't important to me. They are important to you." I had heard this before. This was for me. To help her, but more than that. To help me, but more than that, too. Yet I could not quite fathom what the greater purpose could be.

"You seem to be getting so much better now," I went on. "You are learning so much."

"Yes," she agreed.

"Why are people now so drawn to you? Attracted to you?"

"Because I've been freed from so many fears, and I'm able to help them. They feel some psychic pull to me."

"Are you able to deal with this?"

"Yes." There was no question about it. "I'm not afraid," she added.

"Good, I will help you."

"I know," she replied. "You're my teacher."

Chapter
THIRTEEN

Catherine had gotten rid of her distressing symptoms. She was healthy beyond normal. Her lifetimes were beginning to repeat. I knew we were approaching a termination point, but what I did not realize on this autumn day as she again settled into her hypnotic trance was that five months would elapse between this hypnosis session and her next, which would be her last.

"I see carvings," she began. "Some of them are done in gold. I see clay. People are making pots. They're red . . . some type of red material they're using. I see a brown building, some type of brown structure. That's where we are."

"Are you in the brown building or near it?"

"I'm in it. We're working on different things."

"Can you see yourself while you're working?" I asked. "Can you describe yourself, what you're wearing? Look down. What do you look like?"

"I have some type of red . . . some long red material on. I have funny shoes, like sandals. I have brown hair. I'm working on making some type of figure. It's a figure of a man . . . a man. He has some kind of a stick, a . . . a rod in his hand. The other people are making things out of . . . some out of metals."

"Is this done in a factory?"

"It's just a building. The building's made out of stone."

"The statue that you're working on, the man with the stick, do you know who it is?"

"No, it's just a man. He takes care of the cattle . . . the cows. There are lots of them [statues] around. We just know what they look like. It's a very funny material. It's hard to work on. It keeps crumbling."

"Do you know the name of the material?"

"I don't see that. Just red, something red."

"What will happen to the statue after you make it?"

"It will be sold. Some will be sold in the marketplace. Some will be given to the different nobles. Only those with the finest workmanship will be given to the houses of nobles. The rest will be sold."

"Do you ever deal with these nobles?"

"No."

"Is this your job?"

"Yes."

"Do you like it?"

"Yes."

"Have you been doing this long?"

"No."

"Are you good at it?"

"Not very."

"Do you need more experience?"

"Yes, I'm only learning."

"I understand. Do you still live with your family?"

"I don't know, but I see brown boxes."

"Brown boxes?" I repeated.

"They have little openings. They have a doorway in them, and some of the statues sit inside the door. They're made of wood, some type of wood. We have to make the statues for them."

"What is the function of the statues?"

"They're religious," she answered.

"What religion is there—the statue?"

"There are many gods, many protectors . . . many gods. People are very frightened. There are many things made here. We make games, too . . . game boards with holes in them. Animal heads go in the holes."

"Do you see anything else there?"

"It's very hot, very hot and dusty . . . sandy."

"Is there water around?"

"Yes, it comes down from the mountains." This lifetime was beginning to sound familiar, too.

"Are the people afraid?" I explored. "Are they superstitious people?"

"Yes," she answered. "There's much fear. Everyone is afraid. I'm afraid, too. We must protect ourselves. There is sickness. We must protect ourselves."

"What kind of sickness?"

"Something is killing everyone. Lots of people are dying."

"From the water?" I inquired.

"Yes. It's very dry . . . very hot, because the gods are angry, and they are punishing us." She was revisiting the lifetime with the tannis cure. I recognized the religion of fear, the religion of Osiris and Hathor.

"Why are the gods angry?" I asked, already knowing the answer.

"Because we have disobeyed the laws. They are angry."

"What laws have you disobeyed?"

"Those that have been set down by the nobles."

"How can you appease the gods?"

"You must wear certain things. Some people wear things around their necks. They will help you with the evil."

"Is there a particular god that the people fear most?"

"They're afraid of all of them."

"Do you know the names of any gods?"

"I don't know the names. I only see them. There's one that has a human body but has the head of an animal. There's another one that looks like a sun. There's one that looks like a bird; he's black. They run a rope around their necks."

"Do you live through all this?"

"Yes, I do not die."

"But members of your family do." I remembered.

"Yes . . . my father. My mother is okay."

"Your brother?"

"My brother . . . he's dead," she remembered.

"Why do you survive? Is there something particular about you? Something you've done?"

"No," she answered, then changed the focus. "I see something with oil in it."

"What do you see?"

"Something white. It almost looks like marble. It's . . . alabaster . . . some type of basin . . . they have oil in it. It's used to anoint the heads. . . ."

". . . of the priests?" I added.

"Yes."

"What is your function now? Do you help with the oil?"

"No. I make the statues."

"Is this in the same brown building?"

"No . . . it's later . . . a temple." She looked distressed for some reason.

"Is there a problem there for you?"

"Somebody has done something in the temple that has angered the gods. I don't know. . . ."

"Was it you?"

"No, no. . . . I just see priests. They are preparing some sacrifice, some animal . . . it's a lamb. Their heads are bald.

They have no hair on them at all, nor on their faces. . . ."
She fell silent, and minutes slowly passed. Abruptly she became alert, as if she were listening to something. When she
spoke, her voice was deep. A Master was present.

"It is on this plane that some souls are allowed to manifest
themselves to the people who are still in physical form. They
are allowed to come back . . . only if they have left some
agreement unfulfilled. On this plane intercommunication is
allowed. But the other planes. . . . This is where you're allowed to use your psychic abilities and communicate with
people in physical form. There are many ways to do this.
Some are allowed the power of sight and can show themselves to the people still in physical form. Others have the
power of movement and are allowed to telepathically move
objects. You only go to this plane if it is useful for you to go
there. If you have left an agreement that has not been fulfilled, you may choose to go here and communicate in some
way. But that is all . . . to which the agreement must be
fulfilled. If your life had been abruptly ended, this would be
a reason for you to go to this plane. Many people choose to
come here because they are allowed to see those who are still
in physical form and very close to them. But not everyone
chooses to have communication with these. To some people it
may be too frightening." Catherine fell silent and seemed to
be resting. She began to whisper very softly.

"I see the light."

"Does the light give you energy?" I asked.

"It's like starting over . . . it's a rebirth."

"How can people in physical form feel this energy? How
can they tap into it and be recharged?"

"By their minds," she answered softly.

"But how do they reach this state?"

"They must be in a very relaxed state. You can renew

through light . . . through light. You must be very relaxed so you no longer are expending energy, but you are renewing yours. When you sleep you get renewed." She was in her superconscious state, and I decided to expand the questioning.

"How many times have you been reborn?" I asked. "Have they all been here in this environment, the earth, or elsewhere as well?"

"No," she answered, "not all here."

"What other planes, what other places, do you go to?"

"I have not finished what I have to do here. I cannot move on until I've experienced all of life, and I have not. There will be many lifetimes . . . to fulfill all of the agreements and all of the debts that are owed."

"But you are making progress," I observed.

"We always make progress."

"How many times have you been through lifetimes on the earth?"

"Eighty-six."

"Eighty-six?"

"Yes."

"Do you remember them all?"

"I will, when it is important for me to remember them." We had experienced either fragments or major portions of ten or twelve lives, and, lately these had been repeating. Apparently she had no need to remember the remaining seventy-five or so lifetimes. She had indeed made remarkable progress, at least in my terms. What progress she made from here, from this point, might not depend on the recollection of lifetimes. Her future progress might not even depend on me or my help. She began to whisper softly again.

"Some people touch the astral plane by using drugs, but they do not understand what they have experienced. But they have been allowed to cross over." I had not asked her about drugs. She was teaching, sharing knowledge, whether I asked specifically or not.

"Can't you use your psychic powers to help you progress here?" I asked. "You seem to be developing these more and more."

"Yes," she agreed. "It is important, but not so important here as it will be in the other planes. That is part of evolution and growth."

"Important to me and to you?"

"Important to all of us," she replied.

"How do we develop these faculties?"

"You develop through relationships. There are some with higher powers who have come back with more knowledge. They will seek out those who need the development and help them." She lapsed into a long silence. Leaving her superconscious state, she entered another lifetime.

"I see the ocean. I see a house near the ocean. It's white. The ships come and go from the port. I can smell the seawater."

"Are you there?"

"Yes."

"What is the house like?"

"It is small. It has some type of tower on the top . . . a window where you might look out onto the sea. It has some type of telescope. It's brass, wood and brass."

"Do you use this telescope?"

"Yes, to look for the ships."

"What do you do?"

"We report the merchant vessels when they come into port." I remembered she had done this in another past lifetime, when she was Christian, the sailor whose hand was wounded during a naval battle.

"Are you a sailor?" I asked, looking for confirmation.

"I don't know . . . maybe."

"Can you see what you're wearing?"

"Yes. Some type of white shirt and brown short pants and shoes with big buckles. . . . I am a sailor later in my life, but not now." She could see into her future, but the act of doing so caused her to jump ahead to that future.

"I'm hurt," she winced, writhing in agony. My hand is hurt." She was indeed Christian, and she was again reliving the sea battle.

"Was there an explosion?"

"Yes . . . I smell gunpowder!"

"You will be all right," I reassured her, already knowing the outcome.

"Many people are dying!" She was still agitated. "The sails are torn . . . part of the port side has been blown away." She was scanning the ship for damage. "We must repair the sails. They must be repaired."

"Do you recover?" I asked.

"Yes. It's very difficult to stitch the fabric on the sails."

"Are you able to work with your hand?"

"No, but I'm watching others . . . sails. They're made of canvas, some type of canvas, very hard to stitch. . . . Many people are dead. They have much pain." She winced.

"What is it?"

"This pain . . . in my hand."

"Your hand heals. Go ahead in time. Do you sail again?"

"Yes." She paused. "We are in South Wales. We must defend the coastline."

"Who is attacking you?"

"I believe they are Spanish . . . they have a large fleet."

"What happens next?"

"I just see the ship. I see the port. There are shops. In some of the shops they make candles. There are shops where they buy books."

"Yes. Do you ever go in the book shops?"

"Yes. I like them very much. The books are wonderful . . . I see many books. The red one is with history. They are written about towns . . . the land. There are maps. I like this book. . . . There's a shop where they have hats."

"Is there a place where you drink?" I remembered Christian's description of the ale.

"Yes, there are many," she responded. "They serve ale . . . very dark ale . . . with some type of meat . . . some mutton and bread, very large bread. The ale is very bitter, very bitter. I can taste it. They have wine, too, and long wooden tables. . . ."

I decided to call her by name, to see her responses. "Christian," I called emphatically.

She answered loudly, without hesitation. "Yes! What do you want?"

"Where is your family, Christian?"

"They are in an adjacent town. We sail from this port."

"Who is in your family?"

"I have a sister . . . a sister, Mary."

"Where is your girlfriend?"

"I don't have one. Just the women in the town."

"Nobody special?"

"No, just the women . . . I returned to sailing. I fight in many battles, but I am safe."

"You grow old. . . ."

"Yes."

"Do you ever marry?"

"I believe so. I see a ring."

"Do you have children?"

"Yes. My son will also sail. . . . There's a ring, a ring with a hand. It's a hand holding something. I can't see what. The ring is a hand; it's a hand clasping something." Catherine began to gag.

"What's wrong?"

"The people on the ship are sick . . . it's from the food. We've eaten some food that is bad. It's salt pork." Her gagging continued. I took her ahead in time, and the gagging ceased. I decided not to progress her through Christian's heart attack again. She was already exhausted, and so I brought her out of the trance.

Chapter
FOURTEEN

Three weeks passed before we met again. My brief illness and her vacation had caused the delay. Catherine continued to prosper during this period, but when we began the session, she seemed anxious. She announced that she was doing so well and feeling so much better that she did not feel hypnosis could help her any more than it already had. She was right, of course. Under ordinary circumstances, we might have begun terminating therapy weeks ago. We had continued in part because of my interest in the messages from the Masters and because some minor problems still persisted in Catherine's present-day life. Catherine was nearly cured, and the lifetimes were repeating. But what if the Masters had more to tell me? How could we communicate without Catherine? I knew she would continue our sessions if I insisted. But I did not feel right about insisting. With some sadness, I agreed with her. We chatted about the events of the past three weeks, but my heart was not in it.

Five months drifted by. Catherine maintained her clinical improvement. Her fears and anxieties were minimal. The quality of her life and her relationships was dramatically uplifted. She was dating other men now, although Stuart was still in the picture. For the first time since she was a young child, she felt some joy and real happiness in her life. Occasionally, we would pass each other in the hallway or in the cafeteria line, but we had no formal doctor-patient contact.

Winter passed and spring began. Catherine scheduled an appointment in the office. She had been having a recurring dream about a religious sacrifice of some sort that involved snakes in a pit. People, including herself, were being forced into the pit. She was in the pit, trying to climb out by digging her hands into the sandy walls. The snakes were just below her. At this point in the dream she would awaken, her heart pounding wildly.

Despite the long hiatus, she fell quickly into a deep hypnotic state. Not surprisingly, she was instantly back in an ancient lifetime.

"It is very hot where I am," she began. "I see two black men standing near stone walls that are cold and damp. They have headpieces on. There is a rope around their right ankles. The rope is braided with beads and tassels coming off it. They are making a storage house out of stone and clay, putting wheat in it, some type of crushed grain. The grain is brought in a cart with iron wheels. Woven mats are on the cart or part of it. I see water, very blue. Someone in charge is giving the orders to the others. There are three steps down into the granary. There is a statue of a god on the outside. He has the head of an animal, a bird, and the body of a man. He is a god of the seasons. The walls are sealed with some sort of tar to prevent air from coming in and to keep the grain fresh. My face is itching. . . . I see blue beads in my hair. There are bugs or flies around, making my face and hands itch. I put something sticky on my face to keep them away . . . it smells terrible, the sap from some tree.

"I have braids in my hair and beads in the braids, with gold strings. My hair is dark black. I am part of the royal household. I am there because of some feast. I have come to watch an anointing of priests . . . a festivity to the gods for the coming harvest. There are only animal sacrifices, no humans. Blood from the sacrificed animals runs from a white stand into a basin . . . it runs into the mouth of a serpent. The men wear small gold hats. Everyone is darkskinned. We have slaves from other lands, from across the sea. . . ."

She fell silent, and we were waiting, as if the months had never passed. She seemed to become vigilant, listening to something.

"All is so fast and complicated . . . what they are telling me . . . about change and growth and different planes. There is a plane of awareness and a plane of transition. We come from one life, and, if the lessons are completed, we move on to another dimension, another life. We must understand fully. If we do not, we are not allowed to pass on . . . we must repeat because we do not learn. We must experience from all sides. We must know the side of wanting, but also to give. . . . There is so much to know, so many spirits involved. That is why we are here. The Masters . . . are just one on this plane."

Catherine paused, then spoke with the voice of the poet Master. He was speaking to me.

"What we tell you is for now. You must now learn through your own intuition."

After a few minutes, Catherine spoke in her soft whisper. "There is a black fence . . . within are tombstones. Yours is there."

"Mine?" I asked, surprised at this vision.

"Yes."

"Can you read the inscription?"

"The name is 'Noble': 1668–1724. There is a flower

on it. . . . It is in France or Russia. You were in a red uniform . . . thrown from a horse. . . . There is a gold ring . . . with a lion's head . . . used as an insignia."

There was no more. I interpreted the poet Master's statement to mean there would be no more revelations through Catherine's hypnosis, and this was indeed the case. We were to have no further sessions. Her cure had been complete, and I had learned all that I could through the regressions. The rest, what lay in the future, I had to learn through my own intuition.

Chapter
FIFTEEN

Two months after our last session, Catherine called and scheduled an appointment. She said she had something very interesting to tell me.

When she walked into the office, the presence of the new Catherine, happy, smiling, and radiating an inner peace that made her glow, briefly surprised me. For a moment, I thought about the old Catherine and how far she had come in such a very short time.

Catherine had gone to see Iris Saltzman, a well-known psychic astrologer who specialized in past-life readings. I was a little surprised, but I understood Catherine's curiosity and her need to seek some added confirmation for what she had experienced. I was glad she had the confidence to do this.

Catherine had recently heard about Iris from a friend. She had called and made an appointment without telling Iris about anything that had transpired in my office.

Iris had asked her only for the date, time, and place of her birth. From this, Iris explained to her, she would construct an astrological wheel that, in conjunction with Iris's intuitive gifts, would enable her to discern details from Catherine's past lives.

This was Catherine's first experience with a psychic, and she really didn't know what to expect. To her amazement, Iris validated most of what Catherine had discovered under hypnosis.

Iris gradually worked herself into an altered state by talking and by making notations on the hastily constructed astrological graph. Minutes after she had entered this state, Iris reached for her own throat and announced that Catherine had been strangled and had had her throat cut in a previous life. The throat cutting had been in a time of war, and Iris could see flames and destruction in the village many centuries ago. She said that Catherine had been a young man at the time of his death.

Iris's eyes appeared glazed as she next described Catherine as a young male dressed in a naval uniform, with short black pants and shoes with odd buckles on them. Suddenly Iris grabbed her left hand and felt a throbbing pain, exclaiming that something sharp had entered and damaged the hand, leaving a permanent scar. There were large sea battles, and the location was off the English coast. She went on to describe a life of sailing.

Iris described more fragments of lifetimes. There was a brief life in Paris, where Catherine was again a boy and had died young, in poverty. Another time she was a female American Indian on the southwest Florida coast. During this lifetime she was a healer and walked around barefoot. She was darkskinned and had odd eyes. She would apply ointments to wounds and give herbal medicines, and she was very psychic. She loved to wear blue stone jewelry, a lot of lapis, with a red stone intertwined.

In another lifetime Catherine was Spanish and had lived as a prostitute. Her name began with the letter L. She lived with an older man.

In another life she was the illegitimate daughter of a wealthy father who had many titles. Iris saw the family crest on mugs in the large house. She said that Catherine was very fair and had long, tapering fingers. She played the harp. Her marriage was arranged. Catherine loved animals, especially horses, and she treated the animals better than the people around her.

In a brief lifetime she was a young Moroccan boy who died of an illness in his youth. Once she lived in Haiti, speaking the language and involved in magical practices.

In an ancient lifetime she was Egyptian and was involved in the burial rites of that culture. She was a female with braided hair.

She had several lifetimes in France and Italy. In one, she lived in Florence and was involved with religion. She later moved to Switzerland, where she was involved with a monastery. She was a female and had two sons. She was fond of gold and gold sculpture, and she wore a gold cross. In France she had been imprisoned in a cold and dark place.

In another life, Iris saw Catherine as a male in a red uniform, involved with horses and soldiers. The uniform was red and gold, probably Russian. In yet another lifetime she was a Nubian slave in ancient Egypt. At one point she was captured and thrown into jail. In still another life, Catherine was a male in Japan, involved with books and teaching, very scholarly. She worked with schools and lived to an old age.

And, finally, there was a more recent life as a German soldier who was killed in battle.

I was fascinated by the detailed accuracy of these past-life events as described by Iris. The correspondence to Catherine's own recall while under hypnotic regression was startling— Christian's hand injury while in the naval battle and the description of his clothes and shoes; Louisa's life as a Spanish prostitute; Aronda and the Egyptian burials; Johan, the young raider whose throat was cut by a previous incarnation of Stuart while Stuart's village had burned; Eric, the doomed German pilot; and so on.

There were also correspondences to Catherine's present life. For example, Catherine loved blue stone jewelry, especially lapis lazuli. She was not wearing any, however, during her reading with Iris. She had always loved animals, especially horses and cats, feeling safer with them than with people. And, if she could pick one place in the world to visit, it would be Florence.

By no means would I call this experience a valid scientific experiment. I had no way of controlling the variables. But it happened, and I think it is important to relate it here.

I am not sure what occurred that day. Perhaps Iris unconsciously used telepathy and "read" Catherine's mind, since the past lifetimes were already in Catherine's subconscious. Or perhaps Iris really was able to discern past-life information by the use of her psychic abilities. However it was done, the two of them obtained the same information by different means. What Catherine had arrived at through hypnotic regression, Iris had reached through psychic channels.

Very few people would be able to do what Iris did. Many people who call themselves psychics are merely capitalizing on people's fears as well as their curiosity about the unknown. Today, "psychic" hacks and fakes seem to be coming out of the woodwork. The popularity of books such as Shirley Mac-Laine's *Out on a Limb* has brought forth a torrent of new "trance mediums." Many rove around, advertising their presence locally, and they sit in a "trance" telling an enraptured and awestruck audience such platitudes as "If you are not in harmony with nature, nature will not be in harmony with you." These pronouncements are usually intoned in a voice quite different from the "medium's" own, often tinged with a foreign accent of some sort. The messages are vague and applicable to a wide variety of people. Often the messages deal principally with the spiritual dimensions, which are difficult to evaluate. It is important to weed out the false from the true so that the field is not discredited. Serious behavioral scientists are needed to do this important work. Psychiatrists are necessary to make diagnostic assessments, to rule out mental illness, malingering (faking), and sociopathic (conning) tendencies. Statisticians, psychologists, and physicists are also vital for these evaluations and for further testing.

The important strides that are going to be made in this field will be made using scientific methodology. In science, a hypothesis, which is a preliminary assumption made about a series of observations, is initially created to explain a phenomenon. From there, the hypothesis must be tested under controlled conditions. The results of these tests must be proved and replicated before a theory can be formed. Once the scientists have what they think is a sound theory, it must be tested again and again by other researchers, and the results should be the same.

The detailed, scientifically acceptable studies of Dr. Joseph B. Rhine at Duke University, of Dr. Ian Stevenson at the University of Virginia, Department of Psychiatry, of Dr. Gertrude Schmeidler at the College of the City of New York, and of many other serious researchers prove that this can be done.

Chapter
SIXTEEN

Almost four years have passed since Catherine and I shared this incredible experience. It has changed us both profoundly.

On occasion, she drops into my office to say hello or to discuss a problem that she is having. She has never had the need nor the desire to be regressed again, either to deal with a symptom or to find out how new people in her life may have related to her in the past. Our work is done. Catherine is now free to fully enjoy her life, no longer crippled by her disabling symptoms. She has found a sense of happiness and contentment that she never thought was possible. She no longer fears illness or death. Life has a meaning and purpose for her now that she is balanced and in harmony with herself. She radiates an inner peace that many wish for but few attain. She feels more spiritual. To Catherine, what has happened is all very real. She does not doubt the veracity of any of it, and she accepts it all as an integral part of who she is. She has no interest in pursuing the study of psychic phenomena, feeling that she "knows" in a way that cannot be learned from books or lectures. People who are dying or who have a family member dying often seek her out. They seem drawn to her. She sits and talks to them, and they feel better.

My life has changed almost as drastically as Catherine's. I have become more intuitive, more aware of the hidden, secret parts of my patients, colleagues, and friends. I seem to know a great deal about them, even before I should. My values and life goals have shifted to a more humanistic, less accumulative focus. Psychics, mediums, healers, and others appear in my life with increasing frequency, and I have started to systematically evaluate their abilities. Carole has developed along with me. She has become particularly skillful in death-and-dying counseling, and she now runs support groups for patients dying from AIDS.

I have begun to meditate, something that, until recently, I thought only Hindus and Californians practiced. The lessons transmitted through Catherine have become a conscious part of my daily life. Remembering the deeper meaning of life, and of death as a natural part of life, I have become more patient, more empathic, more loving. I also feel more responsible for my actions, the negative as well as the lofty. I know there will be a price to pay. What goes around truly does come around.

I still write scientific papers, lecture at professional meetings, and run the Department of Psychiatry. But now I straddle two worlds: the phenomenal world of the five senses, represented by our bodies and physical needs; and the greater world of the nonphysical planes, represented by our souls and spirits. I know that the worlds are connected, that all is energy. Yet they often seem so far apart. My job is to connect the worlds, to carefully and scientifically document their unity.

My family has flourished. Carole and Amy have turned out to have above-average psychic abilities, and we playfully encourage the further development of these skills. Jordan has become a powerful and charismatic teenager, a natural leader. I am finally becoming less serious. And I sometimes have unusual dreams.

During the several months after Catherine's last session, a

peculiar tendency had begun to appear during my sleep. I would sometimes have a vivid dream, during which I would either be listening to a lecture or asking questions of the lecturer. The teacher's name in the dream was Philo. Upon awakening, I would sometimes remember some of the material discussed and jot it down. I am including a few examples here. The first was a lecture, and I recognized the influence of the messages from the Masters.

". . . Wisdom is achieved very slowly. This is because intellectual knowledge, easily acquired, must be transformed into 'emotional,' or subconscious, knowledge. Once transformed, the imprint is permanent. Behavioral practice is the necessary catalyst of this reaction. Without action, the concept will wither and fade. Theoretical knowledge without practical application is not enough.

"Balance and harmony are neglected today, yet they are the foundations of wisdom. Everything is done to excess. People are overweight because they eat excessively. Joggers neglect aspects of themselves and others because they run excessively. People seem excessively mean. They drink too much, smoke too much, carouse too much (or too little), talk too much without content, worry too much. There is too much black-or-white thinking. All or none. This is not the way of nature.

"In nature there is balance. Beasts destroy in small amounts. Ecological systems are not eliminated en masse. Plants are consumed and then grow. The sources of sustenance are dipped into and then replenished. The flower is enjoyed, the fruit eaten, the root preserved.

"Humankind has not learned about balance, let alone practiced it. It is guided by greed and ambition, steered by fear. In this way it will eventually destroy itself. But nature will survive; at least the plants will.

"Happiness is really rooted in simplicity. The tendency to

excessiveness in thought and action diminishes happiness. Excesses cloud basic values. Religious people tell us that happiness comes from filling one's heart with love, from faith and hope, from practicing charity and dispensing kindness. They actually are right. Given those attitudes, balance and harmony usually follow. These are collectively a state of being. In these days, they are an altered state of consciousness. It is as if humankind were not in its natural state while on earth. It must reach an altered state in order to fill itself with love and charity and simplicity, to feel purity, to rid itself of its chronic fearfulness.

"How does one reach this altered state, this other value system? And once reached, how can it be sustained? The answer appears to be simple. It is the common denominator of all religions. Humankind is immortal, and what we are doing now is learning our lessons. We are all in school. It is so simple if you can believe in immortality.

"If a part of humankind is eternal, and there is much evidence and history to think so, then why are we doing such bad things to ourselves? Why do we step on and over others for our personal 'gain' when actually we're flunking the lesson? We all seem to be going to the same place ultimately, albeit at different speeds. No one is greater than another.

"Consider the lessons. Intellectually the answers have always been there, but this need to actualize by experience, to make the subconscious imprint permanent by 'emotionalizing' and practicing the concept, is the key. Memorizing in Sunday School is not good enough. Lip service without the behavior has no value. It is easy to read about or to talk about love and charity and faith. But to *do* it, to *feel* it, almost requires an altered state of consciousness. Not the transient state induced by drugs, alcohol, or unexpected emotion. The permanent state is reached by knowledge and understanding. It is sustained by physical behavior, by act and deed, by practice. It is taking something nearly mystical and transforming it to everyday familiarity by practice, making it a habit.

"Understand that no one is greater than another. Feel it. Practice helping another. We are all rowing the same boat. If we don't pull together, our plants are going to be awfully lonely."

On another night, in a different dream I was asking a question. "How is it that you say all are equal, yet the obvious contradictions smack us in the face: inequalities in virtues, temperances, finances, rights, abilities and talents, intelligence, mathematical aptitude, ad infinitum?"

The answer was a metaphor. "It is as if a large diamond were to be found inside each person. Picture a diamond a foot long. The diamond has a thousand facets, but the facets are covered with dirt and tar. It is the job of the soul to clean each facet until the surface is brilliant and can reflect a rainbow of colors.

"Now, some have cleaned many facets and gleam brightly. Others have only managed to clean a few; they do not sparkle so. Yet, underneath the dirt, each person possesses within his or her breast a brilliant diamond with a thousand gleaming facets. The diamond is perfect, not one flaw. The only differences among people are the number of facets cleaned. But each diamond is the same, and each is perfect.

"When all the facets are cleaned and shining forth in a spectrum of lights, the diamond returns to the pure energy that it was originally. The lights remain. It is as if the process that goes into making the diamond is reversed, all that pressure released. The pure energy exists in the rainbow of lights, and the lights possess consciousness and knowledge.

"And all of the diamonds are perfect."

Sometimes the questions are complicated and the answers simple.

"What am I to do?" I was asking in a dream. "I know I can treat and heal people in pain. They come to me in numbers beyond what I can handle. I am so tired. Yet can I say no when they are so needy and I can help them? Is it right to say 'No, enough already?' "

"Your role is not to be a lifeguard" was the answer.

The last example I will cite was a message to other psychiatrists. I awakened about six in the morning from a dream where I was giving a lecture, in this instance to a vast audience of psychiatrists.

"In the rush toward the medicalization of psychiatry, it is important that we do not abandon the traditional, albeit sometimes vague, teachings of our profession. We are the ones who still talk to our patients, patiently and with compassion. We still take the time to do this. We promote the conceptual understanding of illness, healing with understanding and the induced discovery of self-knowledge, rather than just with laser beams. We still use hope to heal.

"In this day and age, other branches of medicine are finding these traditional approaches to healing much too inefficient, time-consuming, and unsubstantiated. They prefer technology to talk, computer-generated blood chemistries to the personal physician-patient chemistry, which heals the patient and provides satisfaction to the doctor. Idealistic, ethical, personally gratifying approaches to medicine lose ground to economic, efficient, insulating, and satisfaction-destroying approaches. As a result, our colleagues feel increasingly isolated and depressed. The patients feel rushed and empty, uncared for.

"We should avoid being seduced by high technology.

Rather, we should be the role models for our colleagues. We should demonstrate how patience, understanding, and compassion help both patient *and* physician. Taking more time to talk, to teach, to awaken hope and the expectation of recovery—these half-forgotten qualities of the physician as healer—these we must always use ourselves and be an example to our fellow physicians.

"High technology is wonderful in research and to promote the understanding of human illness and disease. It can be an invaluable clinical tool, but it can never replace those inherently personal characteristics and methods of the true physician. Psychiatry can be the most dignified of the medical specialties. We are the teachers. We should not abandon this role for the sake of assimilation, especially not now."

I still have such dreams, although only occasionally. Often, in meditation, or sometimes while driving on the highway, or even while daydreaming, phrases and thoughts and visualizations will pop into my mind. These often seem very different from my conscious and usual way of thinking or conceptualizing. They are frequently very timely and solve questions or problems I am having. I use them in therapy and in my everyday life. I consider these phenomena to be an expansion of my intuitive abilities, and I am heartened by them. To me, they are signs that I am headed in the right direction, even if I have a long way to go.

I listen to my dreams and intuitions. When I do, things seem to fall into place. When I do not, something invariably goes awry.

I still feel the Masters around me. I do not know for sure whether my dreams and intuitions are influenced by them, but I suspect so.

EPILOGUE

The book is now completed, but the story goes on. Catherine remains cured, without any recurrence of her original symptoms. I have been very careful about regressing other patients. I am guided by the patient's particular constellation of symptoms and by his or her refractoriness to other treatments, by the ability to be easily hypnotized, by the patient's openness to this approach, and by an intuitive feeling on my part that this is the path to take. Since Catherine, I have done detailed regressions to multiple past lives in a dozen more patients. None of these patients was psychotic, hallucinating, or experiencing multiple personalities. All improved dramatically.

The twelve patients have widely disparate backgrounds and personalities. A Jewish housewife from Miami Beach vividly remembered being raped by a group of Roman soldiers in Palestine shortly after the death of Jesus. She ran a nineteenth-century brothel in New Orleans, lived in a monastery in France in the Middle Ages, and had a distressing Japanese lifetime. She is the only one of the patients other than Catherine who could transmit messages back from the in-between state. Her messages have been extremely psychic. She, too, knew facts and events from my past. She has even more of a facility for accurately predicting future events. Her messages come from a particular spirit, and I am currently in the process of carefully cataloging her sessions. I am still the scientist. All of her material must be scrutinized, evaluated, and validated.

The others were not able to remember much beyond dying, leaving their bodies, and floating to the bright light. None could transmit messages or thoughts back to me. But all had vivid memories of previous lifetimes. A brilliant stockbroker lived a pleasant but boring life in Victorian England. An artist was tortured during the Spanish Inquisition. A restaurant owner, who could not drive over bridges or through tunnels, remembered being buried alive in an ancient Near-Eastern culture. A young physician recalled his trauma at sea, when he was a Viking. A television executive was tormented six hundred years ago in Florence. The list of patients goes on.

These people remembered still other lifetimes as well. Symptoms resolved as the lifetimes unfolded. Each now firmly believes that he or she has lived before and will again. Their fear of death has diminished.

It is not necessary that everyone has regression therapy or visits psychics or even meditates. Those with disabling or bothersome symptoms may choose to do so. For the rest, keeping an open mind is the most important task. Realize that life is more than meets the eye. Life goes beyond our five senses. Be receptive to new knowledge and to new experiences. "Our task is to learn, to become God-like through knowledge."

I am no longer concerned with the effect this book may have on my career. The information that I have shared is far more important and, if heeded, will be far more beneficial to the world than anything I can do on an individual basis in my office.

I hope that you will be helped by what you have read here, that your own fear of death has been diminished, and that the messages offered to you about the true meaning of life will free you to go about living yours to the fullest, seeking harmony and inner peace and reaching out in love to your fellow humans.

ABOUT
THE
AUTHOR

After graduating magna cum laude from Columbia University and receiving his medical degree at the Yale University School of Medicine, Brian L. Weiss, M.D., served his internship at New York University's Bellevue Medical Center and went on to become chief resident, Department of Psychiatry, at the Yale University School of Medicine. Currently, Dr. Weiss is chairman of the Department of Psychiatry at Mount Sinai Medical Center in Miami Beach, Florida, and clinical associate professor, Department of Psychiatry, at the University of Miami School of Medicine. He specializes in the study and treatment of depression and anxiety states, sleep disorders, substance abuse disorders, Alzheimer's Disease, and brain chemistry.

You just learned about past lives in *Many Lives, Many Masters*. Now explore future lives in bestselling author Brian L. Weiss's *Same Soul, Many Bodies*.

Same Soul, Many Bodies

Discover the Healing Power of Future Lives Through Progression Therapy

BRIAN L. WEISS, M.D.

Bestselling Author of *Many Lives, Many Masters*

Just as the lives we've lived previously influence our choices and decisions in this life, what we do in this life influences the lives we are yet to live as we evolve toward immortality. In his revolutionary new book, *Same Soul, Many Bodies*, famed psychiatrist and bestselling author Dr. Brian L. Weiss explores the reality of future-life progression. Using dozens of case histories, Dr. Weiss demonstrates the therapeutic benefits of progression, explaining that because our futures are variable the choices we make now will determine the quality of life when we return. To read *Same Soul, Many Bodies* is a transforming experience that will help you find more peace, joy, and healing in your life's journey.

Available in paperback wherever books are sold.

FREE PRESS
A Division of Simon & Schuster
A VIACOM COMPANY

To learn more about other books by Brian L. Weiss, M.D., visit www.simonsays.com.